Carla Juaçaba

Director and Editor of *2G* Moisés Puente
Graphic design RafamateoStudio
Translation Catarina Chase Aleixo, George Hutton
Proofreading George Hutton
Cover photograph Federico Cairoli
Lithography Rovira Digital, Barcelona
Print agpograf impressors, Barcelona

First published by
Verlag der Buchhandlung Walther und Franz König
Ehrenstrasse 4
D-50672 Köln
verlag@buchhandlung-walther-koenig.de

Printed in Spain
ISBN: 978-3-7533-0258-4

Distribution

Germany, Austria and Switzerland
Buchhandlung Walther König, Cologne
Tel. +49 (0) 221 / 20 59 6-53
Fax +49 (0) 221 / 20 59 6-60
verlag@buchhandlung-walther-koenig.de

Distribution outside the United States and Canada, Germany, Austria and Switzerland
Thames & Hudson Ltd., London
www.thamesandhudson.com

United States and Canada
D.A.P. / Distributed Art Publishers, Inc., New York
www.artbook.com

MIX
Paper from responsible sources
FSC® C104592

Contents

4 **Flip-Flop**
Ana Luiza Nobre

12 **The Discontinuous Architecture of Carla Juaçaba**
María Langarita, Víctor Navarro

18 **House-atelier, Itanhangá**
30 **House in Rio Bonito**
42 **Varanda House, Rio de Janeiro**
54 ***Isostasy*, Mexico City**
58 **Humanidade Pavilion, Rio de Janeiro**
76 **Santa Teresa House, Rio de Janeiro**
90 **Vatican Chapel, Venice Architecture Biennale**
100 ***Ballast*, Venice Architecture Biennale**
106 ***Ministry for All* exhibition, New York**
114 **Videiras House, Rio de Janeiro**
128 **Pedra do Tempo, Lisbon**
132 ***Fil d'air*, Geneva**
136 **Flor de Café, Nepomuceno**

Nexus
141 **A conversation between Eduardo Souto de Moura and Carla Juaçaba**

The Open Space
Exhibition Design
Carla Juaçaba

Ana Luiza Nobre

> Walk as if you are kissing the earth with your feet.
>
> Thich Nhat Hanh

The entire history of architecture could perhaps be reread and rewritten based exclusively on the vertical section, as the history of the encounter between buildings and the ground. Or based on the relationship between the human body and the architectural body, and how they both relate to the horizon line —an expression, as visible as it is intangible, of the Earth's body and the natural laws that govern the planet, ensuring its habitability.

In recent years, this relationship has become increasingly strained due to a set of ethical, theoretical and political issues that have been exacerbated by the grave environmental, urban and political crisis that we are experiencing. Nevertheless, despite these seismic shocks, many architectural works continue to be built

Ana Luiza Nobre is Professor of Theory and History of Architecture at the Catholic University of Rio de Janeiro (PUC-Rio), Brazil.

and celebrated, even though the discipline of architecture itself is deeply mired in the destructive logic of petro-capitalism, devastated rainforests, razed mountains and all the lives destroyed by the colonial-modern project. When compared with anthropology, for instance—which has been deeply affected by non-human life—the extent to which architecture clings onto anthropocentrism and the glorification of the city is astonishing, as if catastrophe were not looming on the horizon. Architecture somehow believes it can remain indifferent to the current crisis, but this crisis is forcing us to alter our views and day-to-day practices, expand our sensibilities and unleash our visual, projectual, urban, political and planetary imagination.

"Where to land?"[1]

Within this context, the above question posed by Bruno Latour, even before the pandemic broke out, is now constantly being asked again. It challenges us to answer how, with what, and with whom we want to live/share/build worlds on this planet, at this dizzying time when "the ground is giving way beneath everyone's feet at once".[2]

The question about a certain fundamental principle of architecture thus gains new meaning: how can we maintain balance on Earth, knowing that this balance is increasingly unstable. Not only in a metaphorical sense, but also because the forces at work can effectively change intensity and direction at any moment. After all, although we do not always remember it, *the Earth moves.*

"It was a beautiful ending"[3]

"Isostasy" is a scientific term, defined as the dynamic gravitational balance between topographic elevations and ocean depths, according to the density of rock masses and tectonic plates, on a geological timescale. It is also the title of an installation by Carla Juaçaba, presented at a small gallery in Mexico City, 2011. This ephemeral and little-known work makes the observer see architecture as physical tension: a mixture of human sweat, forces exerted on matter and the ground, and a confrontation with gravity. Strong magnets, guitar strings, glass marbles supported by rubber washers, metal pulleys and brass profiles (1 × 1 cm) are supported at just four points: together, they are a balancing composition, so fragile that the work collapsed less than a month after its inauguration when an earthquake (magnitude 7.4 on the Richter scale) hit Mexico City. The work, reassembled days later, ended up absorbing the disaster as proof of the idea that architecture is a complex sum of forces that must necessarily equal zero. Otherwise, everything falls apart, perhaps forever.

As with other seemingly weightless and massless works by the architect, this installation in Mexico City also invites us to question the limits of the piece, the physicality, depth and thickness of the elements that comprise it, how they fit together and how they remain stable. We soon realise that there is a horizon of possible

1 — Latour, Bruno, *Down to Earth: Politics in the New Climatic Regime*. Cambridge: Polity Press, 2018. This subtitle refers to the original French edition: *Où atterrir?: Comment s'orienter en politique* (Paris: La Découverte, 2017).

2 — *Ibid.* p. 8.

3 — Carla Juaçaba on her installation *Isostasy*, 2022.

movement, defined in relation to a terrestrial ground —whether in contact with it, towards it or away from it. A ground, therefore, that defines all movement and rest. An experiential ground, unthinkable in Galilean terms: instead, inversely, it references the phenomenological principle sustained by Husserl: *the Earth does not move*.[4]

For this is the ground/floor/Earth that Carla Juaçaba's work invokes. Her work always confronts us with the problem (which is also fundamentally architectural) of the vertical. Not in the sense, though, of the ambition to reach the heights of the Tower of Babel or the skyscrapers of Manhattan or Dubai, but rather in its complementary relationship with the horizontal. In turn, the horizontal is inseparable from the multi-species plane that exists beneath our feet, and from which we are constantly moving further and further away, via shoes, chairs and architecture, as Wellington Cançado notes.[5]

In this sense, what is being outlined, piece after piece, is the project's re-encounter with a telluric dimension that begins with the soles of the feet. An encounter that may be understood, in Bruno Latour's terms, as a "landing", a coming back down to Earth. That is, as a movement that goes against the processes of modernisation/globalisation and the way that they oppose everything rooted in or linked to the ground/soil. As if the prevailing vision (in which modern-rational-scientific knowledge is rooted) were to be replaced by the uncertain horizon of a dancing body. A body which, sooner or later, *inevitably*, falls down.

Hence the strange paradox of Carla's architecture, which is almost a homage to falling. That is, it sees itself as just another body inhabiting Planet Earth and is thus inexorably subjected to the law of gravity. However, it is also lovingly bound to gravity insomuch as it is a force that guides, organises and ultimately guarantees verticality. Without a doubt, as Michel Serres observes, "the real miracle is falling bodies".[6] And even though nobody had thought to come up with a god for gravity, as Serres points out, gravity is surely the only divinity that circulates through Carla's work, in which the structure, swaying and limits of our own body reverberate. A body that sometimes embraces and sometimes defies gravity. When it walks, it loses and regains balance with each step. And when it dances, it throws itself into disorientation and insecurity.

Nothing seems less secure, after all, than the 7,000 supports of Carla's pavilion for Rio+20, the UN Conference on Sustainable Development in Rio de Janeiro. It is a 9,000-square-metre pavilion, and its contact with the ground is almost as fragile as the pieces in the Mexican installation. Although the pavilion has far more supports than the installation, their presence is drastically focused into tiny critical points that threaten to collapse at any moment —and, when seen up close, they seem frighteningly delicate.

The pavillion's programme is what brings stability to the whole. It consists, basically, of exhibition spaces, a library with 10,000 books and a 500-seat auditorium, all distributed within large boxes that balance parallel to the ground. They are entangled

4 — Husserl, Edmund, "La terra não se move", *Periódico Héstia*, vol. 1, no. 01, 2017.

5 — Nobre, Ana Luiza, "Aproximar-se do chão", in Moulin, Gabriela *et al.* (eds.), *Inhabiting the Anthropocene*, Belo Horizonte: BDMG/Cosmopolis, 2022.

6 — Serres, Michel, *The Natural Contract*, Ann Arbor: University of Michigan Press, 1995, p. 72.

within a metal mesh that spreads over the space via the joining of thousands of small industrial components, placed upon a rocky base, with no foundations. It is a vertiginous poetic that explores the limits of safety, avoids the traps set by habit or technical standards, and revels in a game somewhere between precision and improvisation, repetition and invention, choice and chance. This is a 500-tonne scaffolding structure that upholds an idea of lightness, designed by someone who—having Niemeyer's architecture behind her—is aware of the inherent precariousness of making architecture in Brazil, as well as the ephemeral character of her project: after just two weeks, it disappears without a trace.

"A design that you feel from the ground up"[7]

Problems of weight and balance have been recurrent themes in Carla's research ever since one of her first built projects: the Varanda House (2007), which was raised 80 cm above floodable ground in Rio de Janeiro. But, to date, the culmination of this line of enquiry has been the chapel she designed for the Vatican, presented at the Venice Biennale (2018), which barely stands over ditches just 24 cm deep. For what are you meant to do in a sacred grove, on an island opposite the Piazza San Marco, behind a church by Palladio and a Benedictine monastery, where it seems like everything has already been built and imagined? Well, the answer is to do almost nothing. Four steel beams were arranged orthogonally, forming a bench and a cross. And seven concrete ballasts were buried a few centimetres into the ground, as shallow as the waters of Venice —and that's all. There is no inside or outside, no floor, wall or roof. Sometimes, even the built elements blend into the sky and the trees, mirrored within the ultra-polished surface of the steel. But then the absence of limits acquires a cosmic dimension that touches upon the sublime. One experiences an introspection that amounts to a spiritual exercise. The recognition of the human dimension, which is also the recognition of human weakness, is accentuated by the gentle instability of the structure: it looks like it's about to break loose from the ground and join the toing-and-froing of the typically Venetian boats along the Giudecca canal, which mentally cross paths, at all times, with Aldo Rossi's floating theatre.

The laconic design of the chapel is related to the cruciform typology of the Catholic tradition. However, it inverts the Palladian church's sense of monumentality with a freshness that revitalises the search for God. The layout also suggests an analogy with Rossi's design for the cemetery at Modena, and its backbone. A body radically reduced to its skeleton. Purified. Towards the absolute.

The fact that this takes place just a few metres away from Eduardo Souto de Moura's chapel, built with heavy blocks of overlapping solid stone, makes the work all the more significant. The serenity and spirituality that both chapels exude

7 — Carla Juaçaba on the Posse House, 2022.

comes from their exploration of near-opposite procedures in terms of how they relate to the ground. For one of the chapels, its strength comes from the weight and solidity of an architecture that does not hesitate to make holes in the ground: this approach evokes the chapels of northern Portugal that are so rooted in the architect's memory. For the other, the ground itself is valued as part of the design. Here, the ground is not the indistinct backdrop onto which the modernist "object-in-a-field" lies, as with the Niemeyerian palaces of Brasília (1956-60). Nor is the ground inert matter to be freely manipulated on the building site, as in certain geomorphological projects like the Yokohama Maritime Terminal (Foreign Office Architects, 1995-2002). Far from being treated as something prior, a kind of external fatality to be somehow incorporated into the project, the ground here is understood as an element that is not only constitutive but also the very source of architecture, while also being sensitive and intelligible. Hence the care taken with the contact between the building and the earth. For Carla, "the foundation is a drawing—and it should be the first drawing—because it is the first action on a territory, a landscape".[8]

This is not, however, about clinging tight to the site. On the contrary. The relationship between Carla Juaçaba's architecture and the ground can be defined as the soft touch of someone who "kisses the earth with her feet" at each step. It is the simultaneously physical and mental activity of someone who slowly defines, again and again, her own route, with attention and determination. And in doing so, the resonance of a meditative practice from a long tradition intersects with a very specific response, within the framework of contemporary architecture: it echoes the call of the forest amplified by the sweet and firm voice of Ailton Krenak, when he asks us to "tread softly".[9] Because the aim is to forge a relationship with the ground that is not one of domination: instead, it should be a reciprocal relationship, through an architecture concerned about its impact on the planet, without falling into the rhetoric of sustainability or forfeiting the power of the project. In other words, an architecture that shows clear individual authorship, yet also seems to retain a broader, collective bodily memory: it could be something like the near-barefoot walking offered by the most popular footwear in Brazil (the origins of which coincide with the founding of Brasília, in fact): that is, the totally open *rasteirinha*, the flip-flop. It is basically made of a sole and straps of a single material, i.e. a soft and malleable rubber, both fragile and resistant. These flip-flops are lightweight, cheap, flat, easily transportable and available everywhere; they are one of the few commercial products that has managed, up to the present day, to cross the deep social and racial divides that have marked Brazil ever since the colonial period. And they have become irreplaceable in the tropical climate, making it possible to walk on practically any ground (be it a loose surface, like a sandy beach or the mud after a rainstorm, or hot tarmac under the sun). By keeping the walker at a minimal distance from the ground, the flip-flop offers an almost tactile intimacy with it, providing a unique combination of protection, comfort and a sense of freedom. Flip-flops are the polar opposite of the Japanese shoes that inspired the Serpentine Pavilion in London, by Álvaro Siza and

8 — Carla Juaçaba on the Venice chapel, 2022.

9 — Krenak, Ailton, "Spaces to Breathe", Escola da Cidade, 2 August 2020.

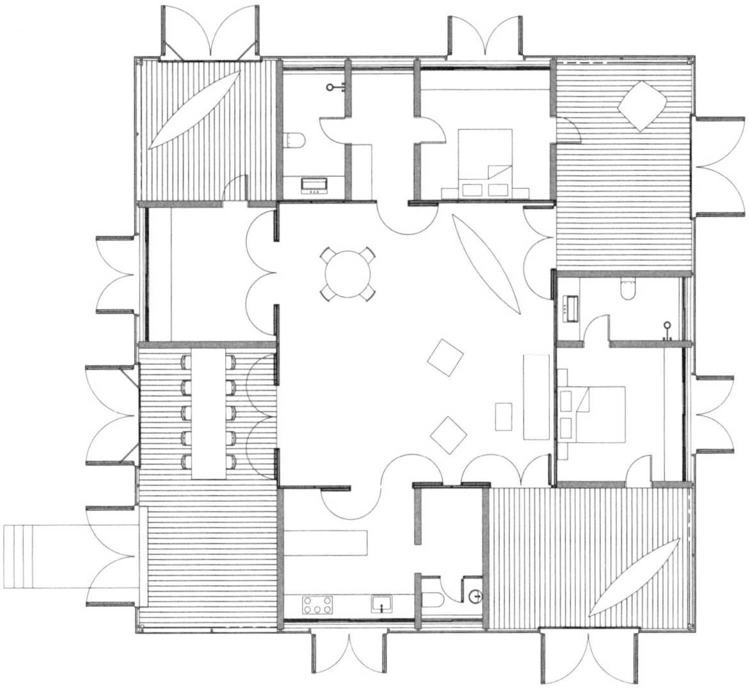

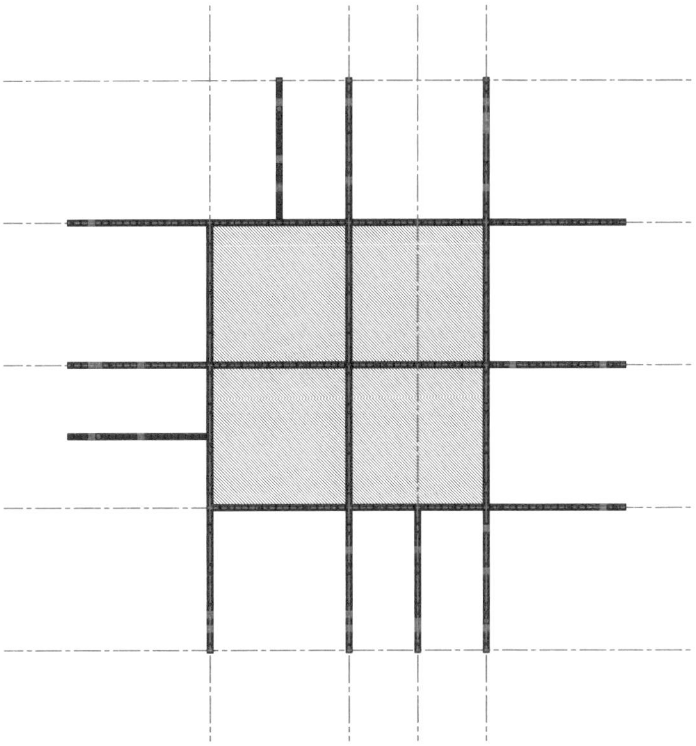

Posse House, Serra de Perópolis, Rio de Janeiro, 2016-

Eduardo Souto de Moura;[10] that is, clogs that only touch the ground at minimal points, despite all the body weight they support.

Little wonder, then, that Carla paid so much attention to the foundations of Posse House, installed amid a rural area of exuberant nature in the mountainous region of Rio de Janeiro. In hard soil plots, "the foundation itself can already be the design of the house", says the architect, "a design that you feel from the ground up".[10] Posse House features a geometric mesh that frames an enclosure at a high elevation, where foundation and structure practically blend into one: the concrete block walls hold two rings of steel beams on their perimeter, one for the floor and the other for the roof. And the programme fits into a single floor, with a central living room around which the bedrooms, bathrooms and kitchen gravitate, with great autonomy. A house that opens up in four directions, which Carla's imagination situates somewhere between a corral and Villa Rotonda.

"A lot of things didn't work out"[11]

Of course, it is not reason, but imagination that is the supreme faculty of the human being. This concept continuously provides material for Carla's architecture, which is wary of any crystallised knowledge and certainly does not confuse drawing with the project itself, nor the future with prediction. What feeds her project design is not-knowing, so to speak. The restlessness of a thought in motion. An imaginative knowledge, wandering, guided by experimentation and by the poetic observation of things. Taking on the risk that comes with the incessant research of materials, techniques and processes, even if this ambition can sometimes prevent the full execution of the project. This was the case in *Ballast*, another proposal for the 2018 Venice Architecture Biennale, in response to the "free space" theme as defined by curators Yvonne Farrell and Shelley McNamara. The work comprises two benches, each 30 metres long, the seats of which are naval ropes, in a nod to the city's history. The supports, meanwhile, are concrete pieces that recall the minimalist sculptures of Robert Morris. Three almost identical prismatic elements, with a single point of stability between them. They are designed to be placed outdoors, in a public space, offering a moment of respite to those bodies exhausted by the monumentality of the exhibition and of the city itself. And, again, it had no foundation, no earthworks. Just a 10 cm steel mesh to prevent the swaying produced by the friction between the ground and the object.[12]

"One action: dismantle"[13]

For Carla Juaçaba, a project is an idea, and a principle of action. Where possible, her approach is based on what she finds at the location. This is true of the Hu-

10 — Álvaro Siza on the Serpentine Pavilion, Faculty of Architecture and Arts, Lusíada University - North (Porto), 5 April 2021.

11 — Carla Juaçaba on Posse House, 2022.

12 — *Ibid.*

13 — The project was carried out within the framework of the Venice Architecture Biennale as a 1:3 scale prototype in the Giardini delle Vergini.

manidade Pavilion, which, according to the architect, "was already there" —she is referring to both the material (i.e. the scaffolding that is continuously being put up and taken down for events at the Copacabana Fort) and the landscape itself, a rocky promontory that juts into the sea, on the border area between the city and the Atlantic horizon. The same can be said of the Ministry for All (2020), an imaginary political structure in Brasília reconciled with the sense of democracy; purely and simply, one more Niemeyerian prism would be installed upon a still-unoccupied part of the triumphal Esplanade of Ministries that so defines Brasília's architectural and urban profile.

On a very different scale, such a sense of economy is reformulated in a more recent intervention at New York's Storefront gallery (designed by Vitto Acconci and Steven Holl), a legendary point of confluence between art and architecture. No design. No additions. Just the decision to dismantle and strip down, one by one, the characteristic rotating panels on the façade. This was followed by the surprising discovery of so many patched-up repairs, suddenly made visible: the project exposed the irrationality of construction processes which are so often covered up by impeccable finishes, as well as the very contradictions of which architecture is made.

Knowledge cannot be separated from experience, Carla seems to tell us. And suddenly, it is as if we hear the spectral voice of Alberto Caeiro:

> All the opinions ever formed about Nature
> Never made a flower bloom or a blade of grass grow
> All the knowledge there is of things
> Was never something I could seize, like a thing.
> If science aspires to be true,
> What truer science than that of things without science?
> I close my eyes, and the reality of the hard earth I'm lying on
> Is so real that even the bones in my back feel it.
> Where I have shoulder blades I don't need reason.[1]

14 — Carla Juaçaba on her intervention at the Storefront Gallery, 2022.

15 — Caeiro, Alberto, "Todas as opiniões que há sobre a natureza", in *Poemas Inconjuntos*, Lisbon: Presença, 1994. This translation is taken from Pessoa, Fernando, *A Little Larger Than the Entire Universe: Selected Poems*, London: Penguin Books, 2006.

María Langarita, Víctor Navarro

In *How to Write a Thesis*, Umberto Eco claims that it is possible to lay the groundwork for an academic research project from absolutely anywhere, regardless of how far away this place is from the centres of knowledge. Even if there is very little reference material available there, it can still be enough to work up the desired academic text. From a small town in Montferrat, Italy, Eco himself set out to prove that he could write a doctoral thesis about "the concept of metaphor used by Italian baroque treatise authors", referring only to the material found on the shelves of the municipal library. In the book, he tells future (and probably sceptical) PhD students about the steps he takes to carry out this task.

This present text could also be considered proof—the reader will judge its validity—of Eco's conjecture,

María Langarita (1979) holds a PhD in architecture from the Universidad Politécnica de Madrid (UPM), and is currently lecturer in projects at the Madrid School of Architecture (ETSAM); **Víctor Navarro** (1979) holds a PhD in architecture from the UPM, and is lecturer in projects at ETSAM. He has also taught at Harvard University's Graduate School of Design (GSD). Since 2005, they have been working together in the architecture studio Langarita Navarro, based in Madrid. Their work has won a range of international prizes, such as a Special Mention for emerging architects at The European Union Prize for Contemporary Architecture - Mies van der Rohe Awards (2013), for their project for the Red Bull Music Academy in Madrid. Their work has also been featured in numerous publications, including their own monographic issue of the magazine *2G* (no. 70, 2014).

i.e. that it is possible to put forward a theory on certain architectures from a distance, without having set foot inside them. Here, we are using only the information gleaned from photographs, drawings, or what we have learnt from our own conversations with Carla Juaçaba. Sadly, the closest we've ever been (in time and space) to a work of hers was in Mexico City, a few weeks before she installed her piece *Isostasy* (2012) at LIGA. We were disappointed we didn't get to see it, although perhaps we were lucky, depending on how you look at it: an earthquake toppled the exhibition not long after it opened. The work was so delicate that it collapsed in the first jolts of the quake. Those fortunate enough to visit it in person were met with a levitating installation, made up of stacks of precious materials in their everyday manifestations: marbles, rubber washers, rods, brass tubes, a stone ballast, magnets and, most importantly, an eerie gap, five centimetres high, that drew a horizon of air right across the room. The precise arrangement of the varied materials meant that, against all odds, the installation stayed standing, in balance. Right there, an elemental magic trick was being played out; Juaçaba had cleverly harnessed the properties of each material to piece together a kind of floating pentagram. Between the objects, a set of elemental forces—like gravity, friction and magnetism—were activated, and they worked in such a way that the materials did not need to be joined by any chemical or mechanical means. With *Isostasy*, Juaçaba was implicitly presenting a manifesto on adjacency and balance, although she did not put it in those words. Essentially, she was making the point that it is possible to produce a discontinuous architecture. This claim might seem slight, or perhaps just a smart quip, but deep down it is a radical reflection on how we handle the world's material, and how the world is built. Seemingly arbitrary decisions, such as determining whether motorists should drive on the left or the right side, can have a profound impact on the land and its inhabitants; similarly, the prerogative to roll out discontinuous architecture in the world thus defines its modes of transformation.

If the aim is to build a stable entity, any amalgamation of disparate materials must be united by various binding forces in order to bring stability to the structure as a whole. More often than not, a wide range of constructive solutions are used, i.e. different techniques for soldering, sticking, joining and adhering. The result could be called "chemical architecture", in which case the material ends up forming compounds, i.e. new groupings that have undergone reactive binding processes, giving rise to continuous architecture. Thereafter, this new material must be subjected to a complex process if it is to be decomposed again. The borders between the incorporated elements become blurred, sometimes even indiscernible. In David Bestué's piece *Transition from Plastic to Wood* (2013), the Spanish artist set himself the unique task of transmuting a white-coloured polymer into the cellulose fibres of a log. The two pure ends of the piece's symbolic arch gradually contaminate each other the closer they get to the keystone. The piece becomes materially ambiguous around the centre of the arch. Bestué creates a kind of mythological material that poses the same scientific dilemma as in the transitioning of the bodies of the minotaur, the griffin, the chimera or the centaur. This continuity is conceptually prob-

Friedrich Justin Bertuch,
Bilderbuch für Kinder, 1790-1830.

David Bestué, *Transition from Plastic to Wood*, 2013.

lematic, yet very common within conventional building processes: solders, mortars, silicones and other binding solutions serve to join, cover, encase or hybridise some materials with others. Composites, i.e. synthetic materials mixed together in varied ways to form a compound, are being used more and more. Even non-composites end up behaving like composites in the construction process of any given project. We could say that Bestué's piece, *Transition from Plastic to Wood*, is the antithesis of Carla Juaçaba's approach. In her work, the Brazilian architect aspires to produce a discontinuous architecture instead, in which each object is always the reflection of its own finiteness, and in which any juxtaposition serves to assert the independence of each element from the others. Juaçaba positions herself beside other likeminded creators (or vice versa), such as the Mexican artist José Dávila. They arrange their works like an ingenious game of balancing, using diverse bodies. They explore the properties of each material, in order to "summon" them to do something that is in fact inherent to them: the elastic materials are set to work on traction, while the dense or solid ones are used for compression. Those that can stand being bent are used for cantilevers, and the heavy materials serve to weigh down the whole operation. In these works, the spectator's visual pleasure goes hand-in-hand with a built-in concern for their imminent collapse.

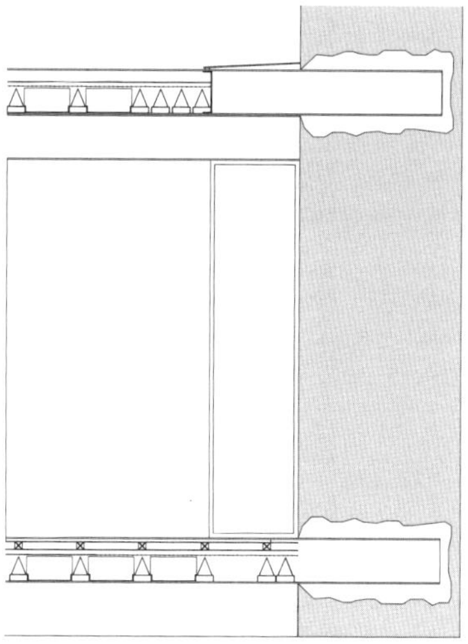

Carla Juaçaba, Rio Bonito House, 2004-2005.
Detail of the metal girders inserted within the stone walls.

We were saying earlier that the installation *Isostasy* is a manifesto, and perhaps now it can be understood more clearly. In the installation, Juaçaba managed to create an architecture without the use of any chemical elements: she makes the most of nature's basic forces, via the intelligent use of the materials' own properties. The way the installation was brought to an abrupt end also shows us the fragility and limitations that this kind of architecture must take into account. Of course, if the approach used for *Isostasy* were applied to a conventional building, it would be seen as reckless at the very least, or even condemned as a criminal act in a court of law. No wonder, then, that conventional architecture uses other systems for binding and adhering.

Juaçaba herself is no stranger to these issues. In Rio Bonito House, one of her first works, the metal girders that support the roof are inserted within two strong, parallel stone walls. The structure seems to be held up by gravity alone; however, hidden inside is poured concrete, which secures the connection between the two constructive elements. We have heard Juaçaba criticising this detail, saying that she wishes she'd come up with a different solution, lamenting that she should have done it "better". We can infer that her vexation comes from having given in, at a time of great pressure, to the "easy" solution of concrete, rather than managing to create a discontinuous support structure. In fact, for all intents and purposes, the girder does actually look like it sits cleanly upon the wall; not many would be able to fathom how it was really done. But Juaçaba is not the kind of architect who cares about appearances: she is more interested in substance. And, in this particular case, to her frustration, concrete is the substance.

The fact that Juaçaba comes from the Brazilian architecture tradition makes her reticence to use concrete, as a building material, all the more surprising. When looking over her work, it's hard to find projects that showcase the material quality of poured concrete. This refusal itself becomes a distinguishing feature. Juaçaba has been known to boast—though perhaps the word is too strong—of having managed to avoid, on several occasions, the use of traditional foundations, i.e. the pouring of fresh concrete onto the ground to create a homogenous support structure. This technique is frequently used to prevent differential settlements, whereby the construction can end up with large cracks, or, in the worst-case scenario, completely collapsing. For Juaçaba, what she achieved in the imposing, temporary Humanidade Pavilion—a set of huge boxes, levitating within a cubic cloud of scaffolding—was a triumph. This time, *Isostasy*'s invisible magnetic field was transformed into a visible forcefield, in which hundreds of vectors crossed the huge platform on Fort Copacabana. Much to Juaçaba's relief, there were so many points of support that, despite the enormous scale of the artifact, there was no need to create new foundations. Her relief wasn't so much about avoiding the use of concrete: it was more about the fact that, once the exhibition was over, the installation could be removed without leaving behind any trace. She further reasserted, thus, the discontinuity between her architecture and the ground that it stands on.

At this point, some readers will be frowning in bemusement: but Juaçaba *does* use concrete, they'll be thinking. They're right, of course: to shun it completely would impose a near-impossible restriction, an extremely complex one in terms of the construction process. But, as we see it, Juaçaba feels more comfortable when using prefabricated concrete, almost like an *objet trouvé* far removed from the building context. She appears to understand the ground (upon which the work is built) as just another entity in her architectural games of balancing materials, keeping them separate. That's why the terrain and the construction should be understood as independent elements; they should not contaminate each other, but rather maintain their discontinuity. In her elemental Vatican Chapel on the island of San Giorgio Maggiore, as part of the Venice Biennale of Architecture, Juaçaba insists on this strategy. A set of concrete crossbeams, separated equidistantly, mediates between the garden and the angular stainless-steel structure, which is simultaneously a crucifix and a bench. Here, the concrete parts are a mediating object, much like the rubber washers in the piece *Isostasy.*

Despite the fact it worked for the Chapel, a similar technique did not work in the Venice Giardini, at the same Biennale. The piece *Ballast*—imagined as a long bench made up of thirty-metre cables, supported by prefabricated concrete sculptures to act as ballasts—did not come to fruition. For those not quite so familiar with how structures behave, the steeper the curve of the catenary, the greater the horizontal force must be in order to counteract it. In this case, given that there were no proper foundations, the friction of the ground was the only thing holding the concrete blocks in place. Perhaps the calculations flagged up a problem, or maybe it failed a loadbearing test; either way, it was decided that the installation could not go ahead as planned. Once again, Juaçaba's radical exploration collapsed, but this time even before the public got to see it. The piece, as it had been designed, was not viable. Juaçaba, instead of searching for a traditional solution—such as by creating foundations in which the terrain and the concrete block would function as one, joined as a single unit—opted to leave the installation as it was, in its unfinished state. She decided that it was better to give up, rather than pumping chemicals into the ground and thus producing a compound in continuity. Some might claim that Carla Juaçaba's position is a nostalgic one, strangely distanced from the new times we are living in; they might claim that the cyborg condition we've reached is part of an inevitable process; that material purity is a fallacy; that it's impossible to escape from this synthetic, artificial world in which everything can be understood as a compound. However, on the other hand, we can see in her defiant stance a strong commitment to the world's material production. Her work looks into how objects' potential capacity for change and becoming transformed might be conserved. The direct application of material, with no added processes; the commitment to basic local production without heavy industry or repurposing, which is being harmed by the complex decomposing processes involved in high energy consumption —these procedures could be more common if, as Carla Juaçaba shows us, we were more willing to engage with and uphold discontinuous architecture.

House-atelier, Itanhangá

2000-01

This sloping site in Itanhangá has an irregular topography, as well as developed vegetation that has been totally preserved. The construction of this house-atelier created generous spaces with large openings to the outside, in an attempt to get closer to nature.

The house, with its metallic structure, has a reinforced slab roof over galvanised aluminium tiles covered with expanded clay. The building's dual function—house and atelier—meant dividing the area into two spaces, i.e. the double-height atelier and then the residence over two levels: the living room and kitchen are located downstairs, while the bedroom and veranda, overlooking the garden, are upstairs. The doors of the atelier are made of taquara (a kind of bamboo) sewn onto a steel structure, and they slide and rotate, functioning as *brises-soleis*. In the kitchen, the wall is a retaining wall; it is formed into shelves and made from raw stone extracted from the site itself. The internal dividing walls are made of reinforced mortar, while the external ones are made of brick; both have plastering made of gravel and Xadrez powder. The interior walls can be moved, and are structured with double MDF: they divide the environment, while also offering well-integrated spaces, amplitude and wellbeing.

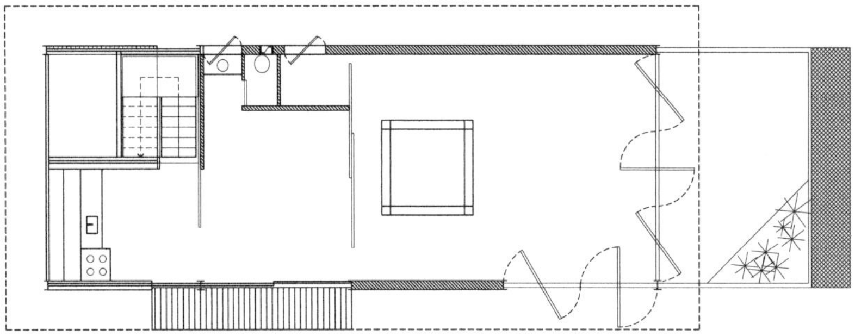

Ground floor

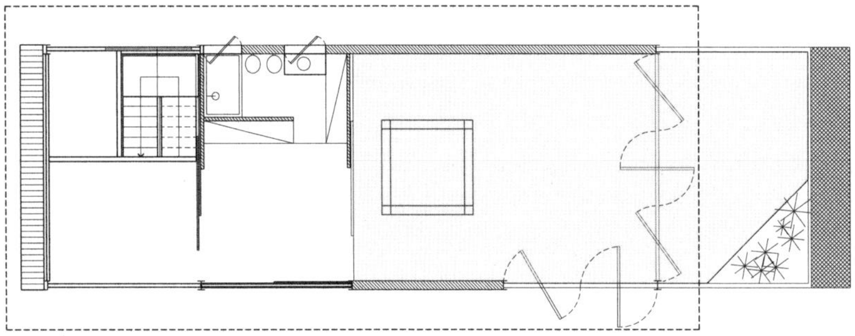

First floor

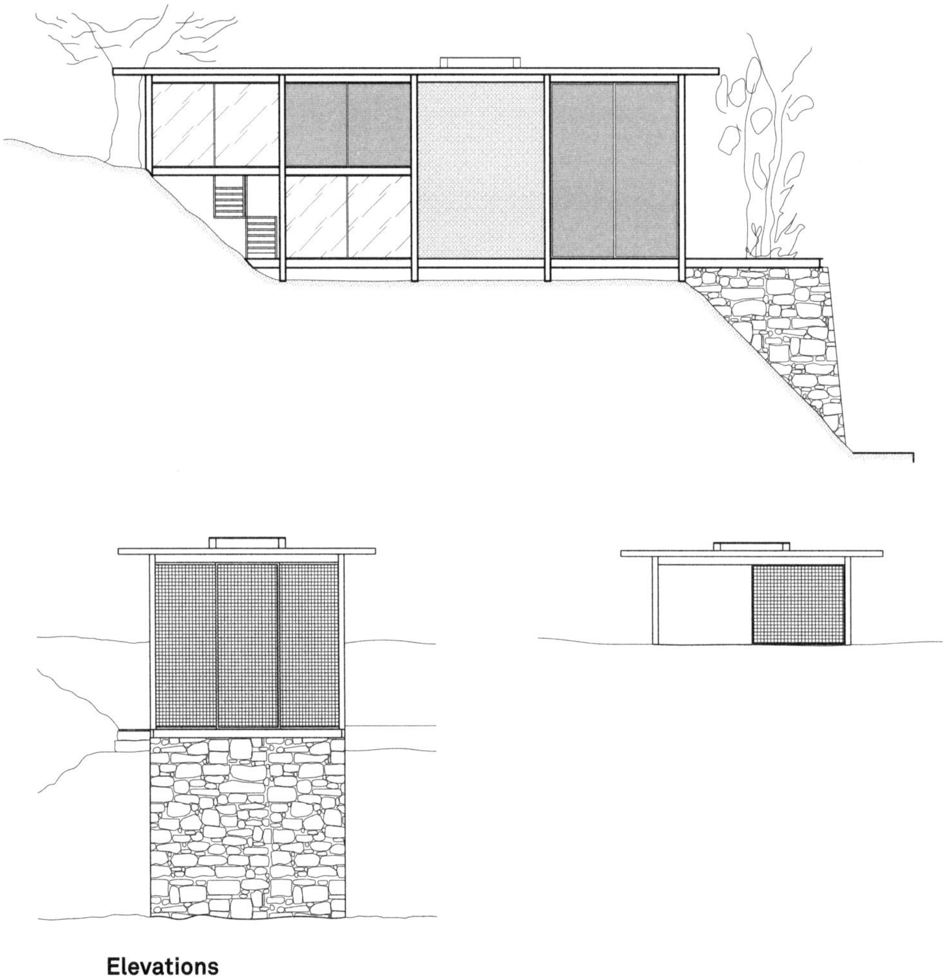

Elevations

House-atelier, Itanhangá

House-atelier, Itanhangá

House-atelier, Itanhangá

House in Rio Bonito

2004-05

This weekend house is located in a mountain area east of Rio de Janeiro. The site is near a river, which was a key factor when choosing this location.

Two bearing walls made of stone, each 110 cm thick, support four steel beams that hold the roof and floor joists. Two voids break through the roof at each end of the structure: these gaps let in a great deal of light, shining down on the stone bearing walls. This creates a striking contrast between the heaviness of the structure and the lightness of the roof and floor, which float above the rough ground.

On the front façade, the floor-to-ceiling glazing offers views of the river. Meanwhile, the openings on the rear façade give vertical continuity to the large openings above. As the house is suspended from the ground, it is protected from moisture and the weather, while maintaining a visual connection to the river. The structural stone walls are pathways to a roof garden outside, and they contain a fireplace and wood stove inside. Water and fire, weight and lightness, the archaic and the modern —they all coexist in the cosmology of this habitat.

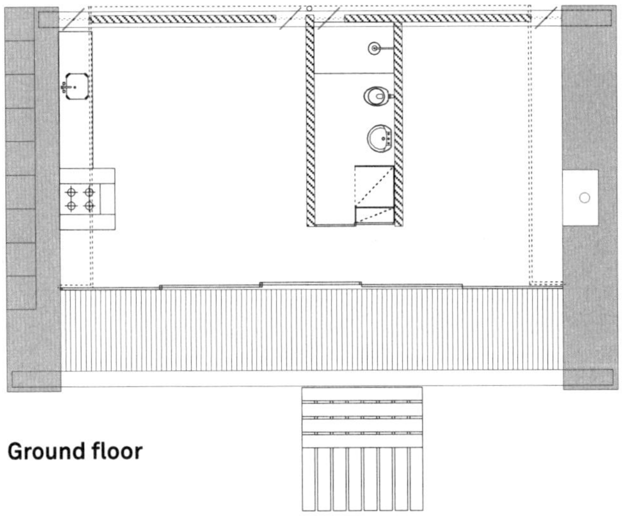

Ground floor

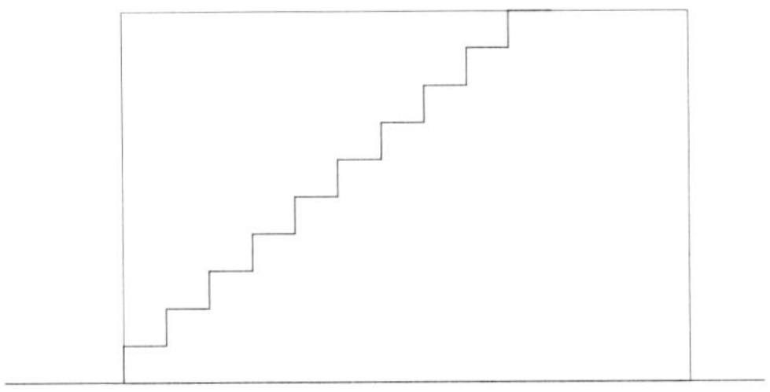

Side elevation

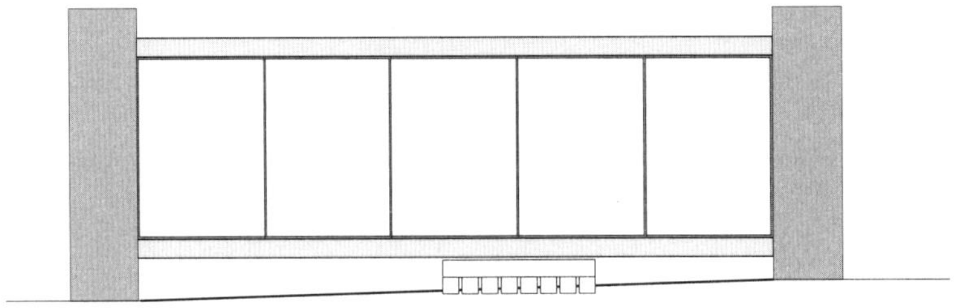

Front elevation

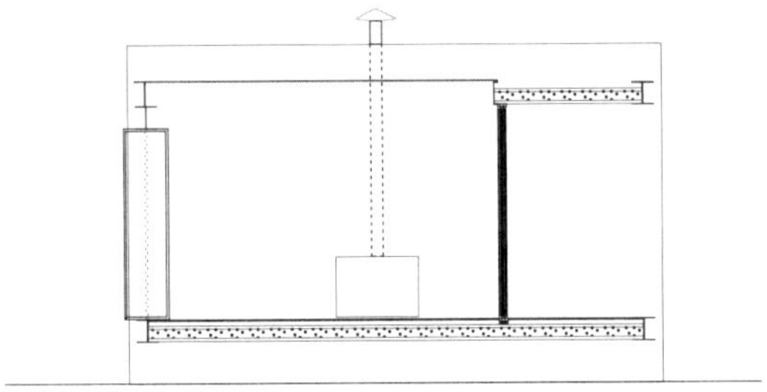

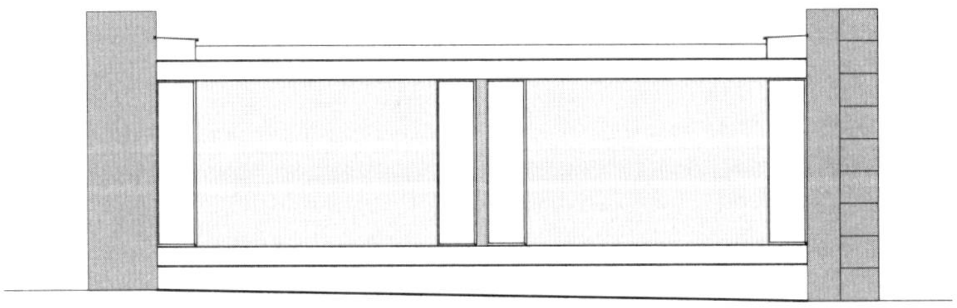

Back elevation

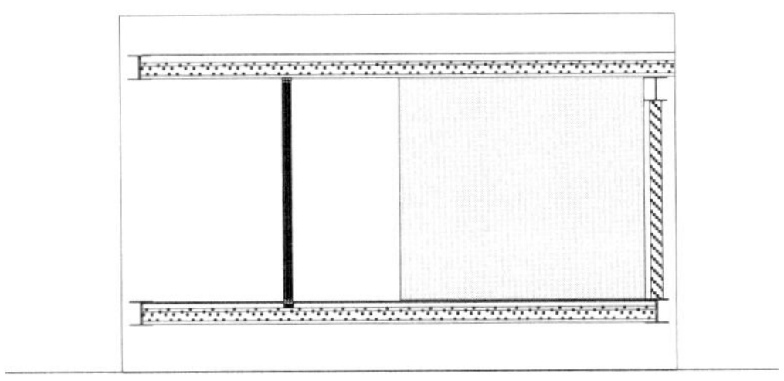

Cross-sections

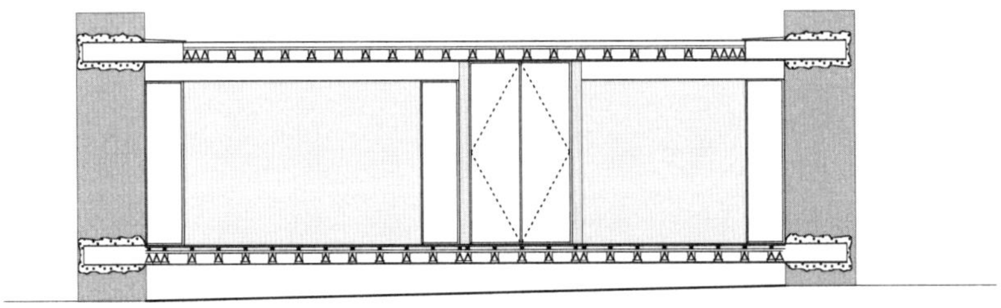

Longitudinal section

House in Rio Bonito

Varanda House, Rio de Janeiro

2007-08

This house is built on the continuous border between the nature and the city of Rio de Janeiro. The centennial trees were the only pre-existing element on site, and the place was so beautiful that there was an urge to leave it untouched, or design a house with less presence. In the end, the house split the site into two lengths, and the reduced presence, as desired, had to be very incisive. The skylight (24 × 0.6 metres) is an opening that accentuates that division.

The view goes beyond the house; the parallel walls, solid and white, do not interrupt it. The living room is in the middle, with the other rooms alongside it. The centre of the house can become an open terrace. Brazilian housing usually has a terrace area as the most important place, and in this case, it is already built-in. The roof juts out 1.5 metres beyond the glass: this way, the windows can be opened when it is raining, which is very important in our climate. What brings intimacy to this glasshouse is its immersion in nature. The light that passes by, calmly, throughout the day, is cast onto the parallel white walls.

Given the geography of the site, which lies beneath the mountain and is vulnerable to flooding, the floor is suspended 80 centimetres above the ground. The steel structure was built in two weeks; the sandwiched zinc-aluminium roof tiles were installed in just one day.

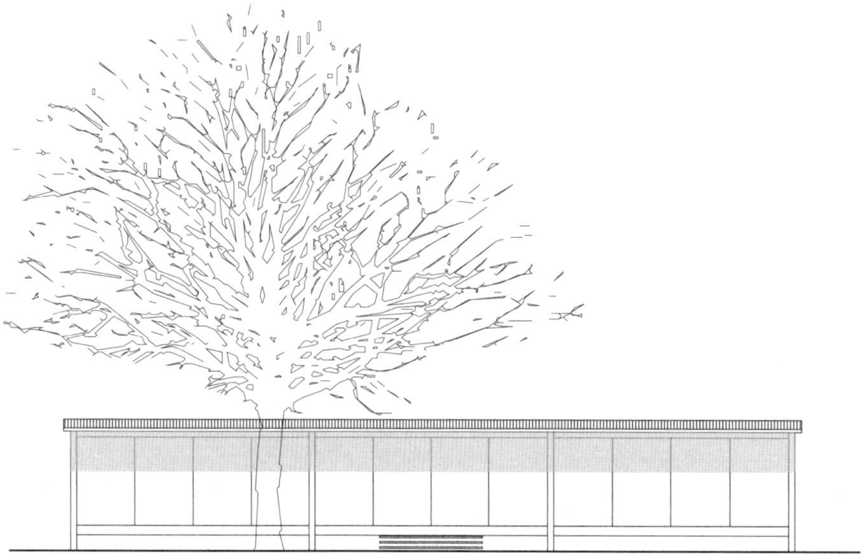

Elevation

Section

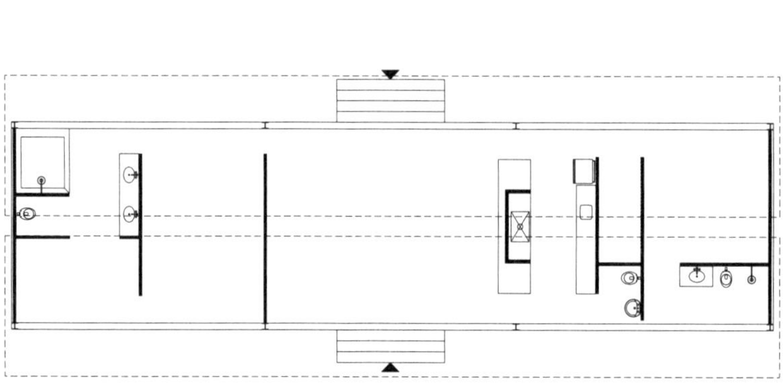

Ground floor

Varanda House, Rio de Janeiro

Isostasy, Mexico City

2012

This installation for LIGA—an independent platform founded in Mexico City in 2011, that promotes contemporary Latin American architecture—is based on the idea that all architecture is a physical effort: the task of building entails work, force exerted on matter and the introduction of an abstract conception into the context of the terrain. Strong magnets, guitar strings, green glass marbles, metal pulleys and small brass strips create a balancing composition that alludes to structural situations like other ones constructed by the architect. This installation highlights almost telluric physical tensions, with which architecture orders material and confronts gravity. It is about the probity and beauty of the materials. There is an apparent tranquillity and calmness to this object, but it is not true: in order for it to stay standing, immense effort and a high level of entropy is required. However, we remain oblivious to all this effort: it is never actually seen in architecture.

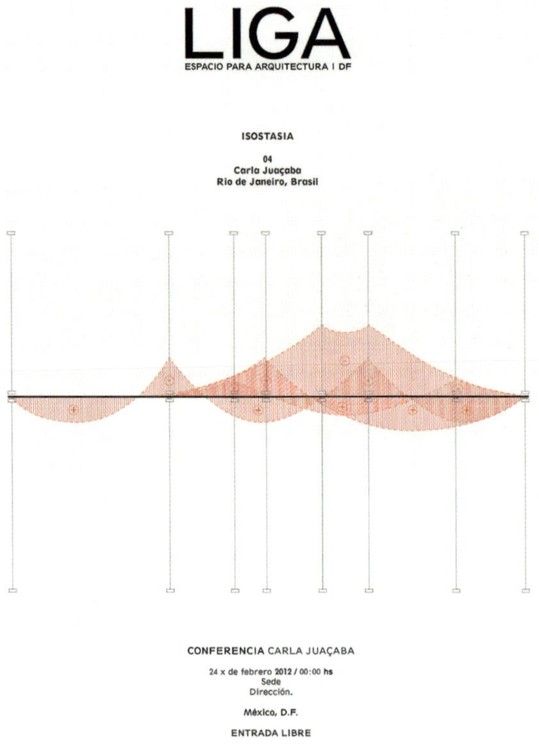

The work's title, *Isostasy*, refers to the ideal gravitational equilibrium that regulates the height of continents and the depths of oceans, according to the density of rock-like masses. The term was first coined in 1889, when the geographer Clarence Edward Dutton described this phenomenon in terms of the hydrostatic equilibrium of tectonic plates. In a twist of fate, as if the architect had planned it in advance, and in direct relation to the title of the show, this fragile installation collapsed on 20th May 2012: just 25 days after the show's inauguration, an earthquake measuring 7.4 on the Richter scale shook Mexico City. Even though the incident caused some losses, the work—which so precisely expressed the fragility of a construction in equilibrium—was fully restored a few days later.

Humanidade Pavilion, Rio de Janeiro

2012

The Humanidade Pavilion was a temporary building made for Rio+20, the international conference on sustainable development. This project was designed together with the theatre director Bia Lessa, and it consisted of a scaffold building, translucent, exposed to all weather conditions: light, heat, rain, the sounds of waves and the wind, thus reminding human beings of their frailty when compared to the might of nature. The structure itself was composed of five structural walls, 170 metres long and 20 metres high, with 5.4 metres in between them. This created a suspended walkway over Rio de Janeiro's landscape, interrupted when necessary by spaces intended for reflection and thought.

The exhibitions rooms act as bracing for the whole structure, strengthening it. Scaffold is the only material that we know of that can support such a weight, and through which rain and wind can pass. One of the main goals in architecture, with regards to sustainability, is to build with what you have at hand. The materials used here are sustainable: everything is 100% reusable.

The project was made from reused materials. Scaffolding is moved on from its usual role, as support structure, to become a building all by itself —and then other projects in the future.

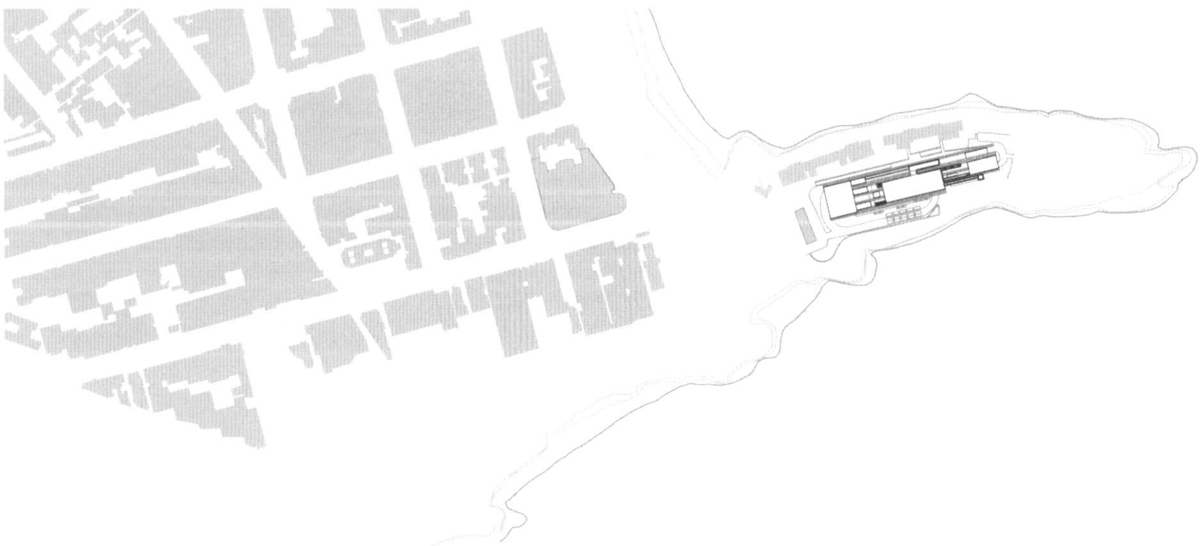

LINGU
OTIMISMO
//HU
MANI

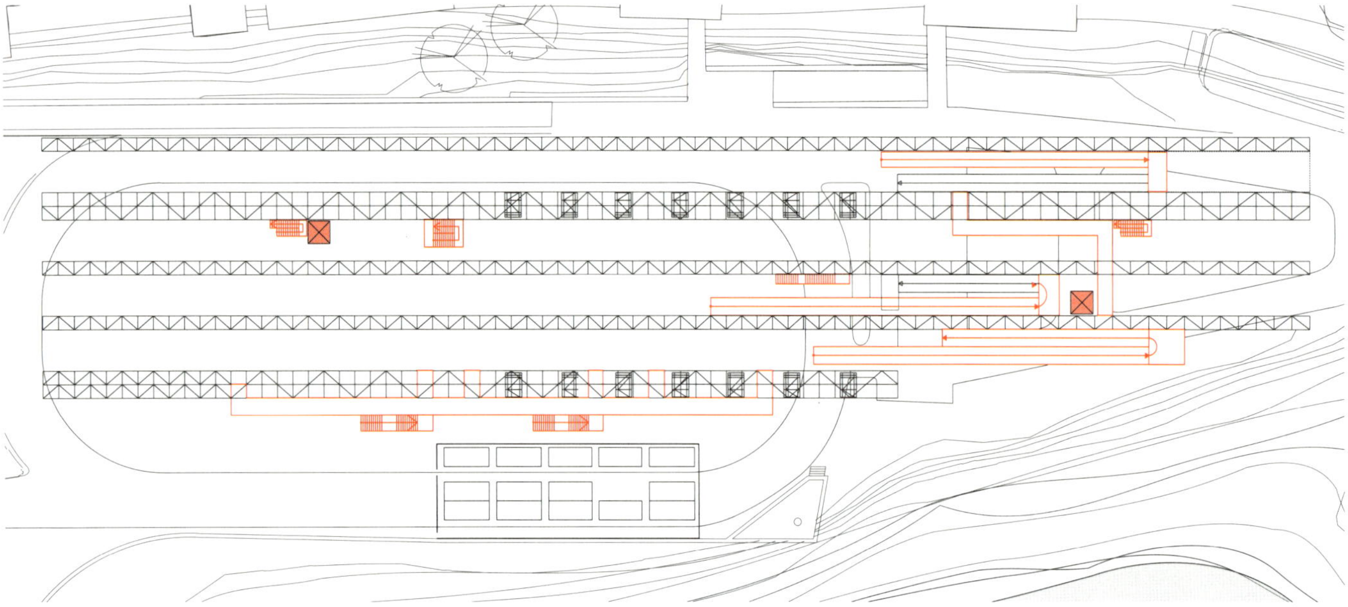

Ground floor

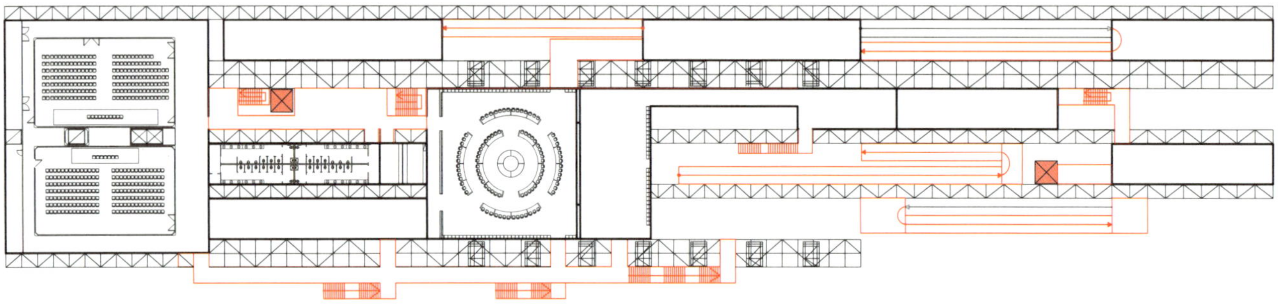

First floor

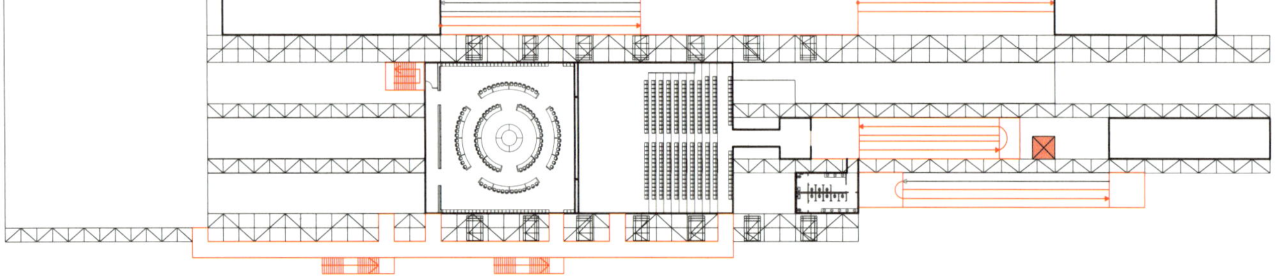

Second floor

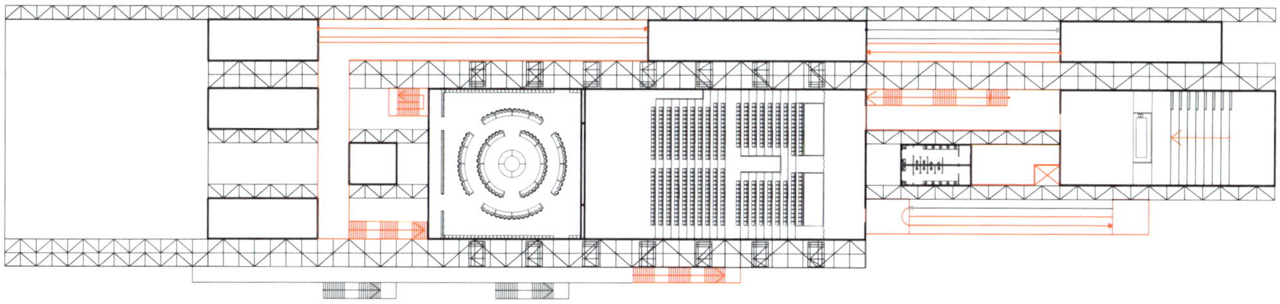

Third floor

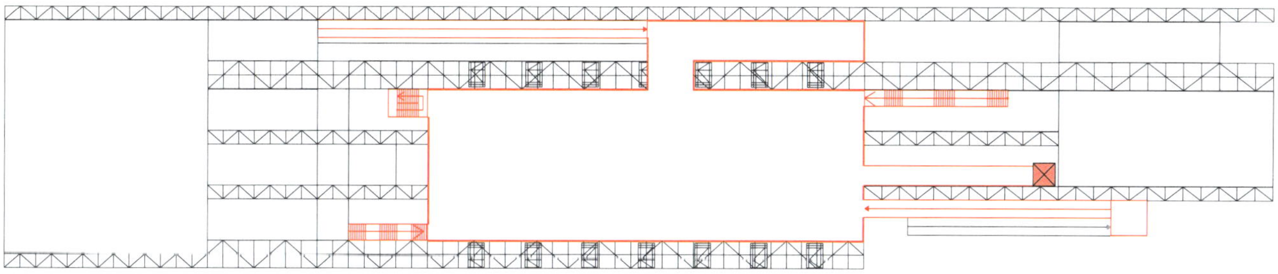

Fourth floor

NGUAS
FORMAR O FUTURO.

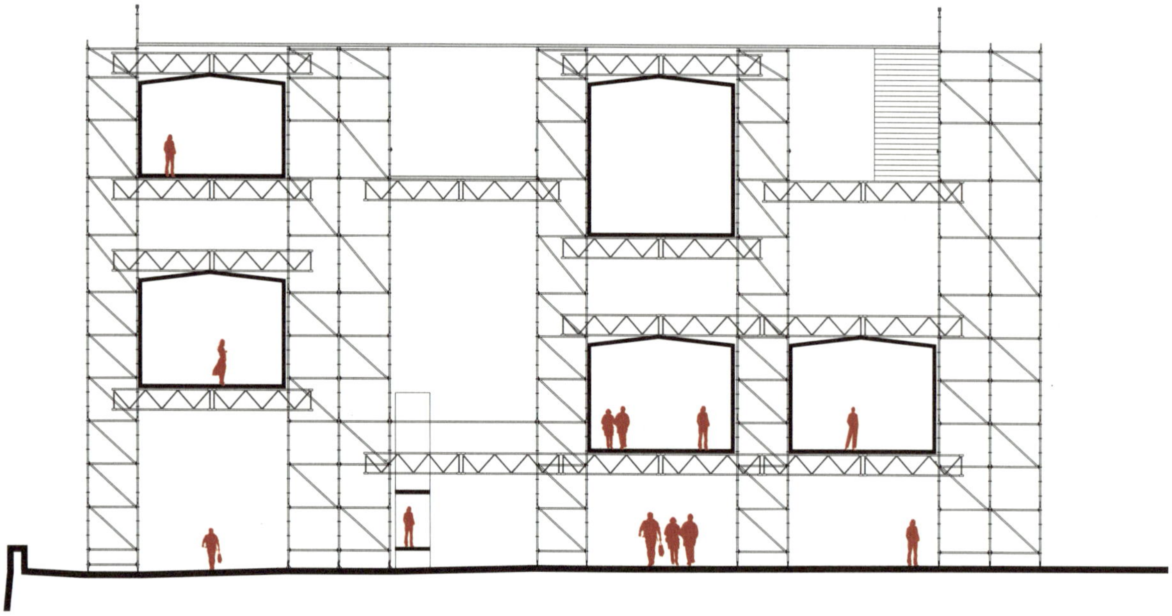

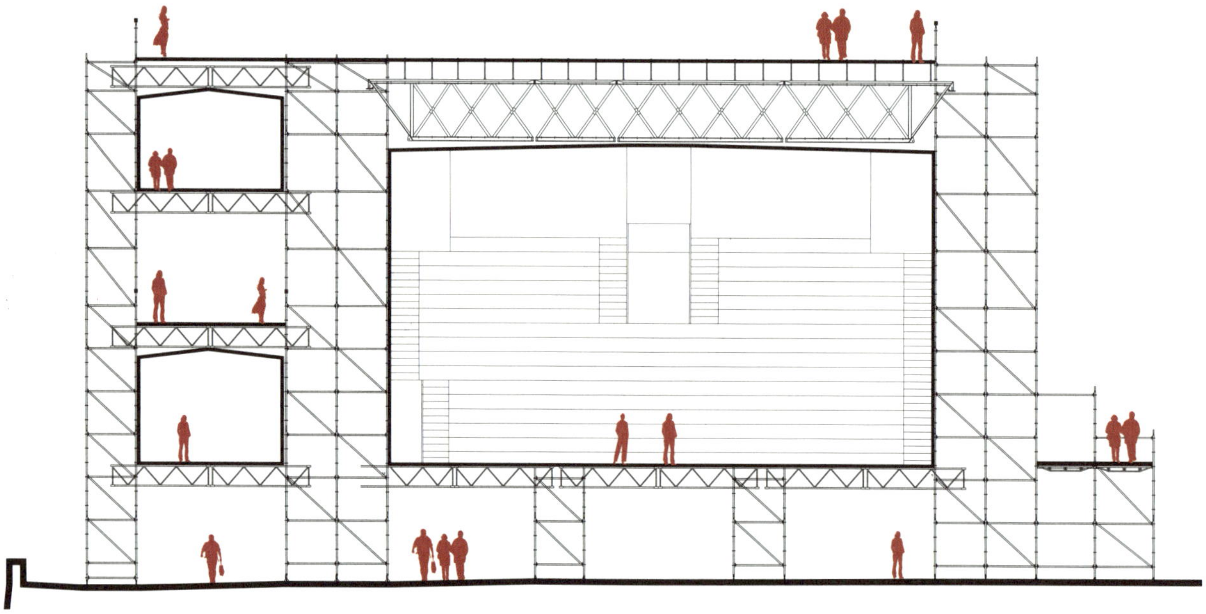

Cross-sections

Humanidade Pavilion, Rio de Janeiro

BIODIVERSIDADE
BRASILEIRA

O HOMEM
E SUAS CONEXÕES

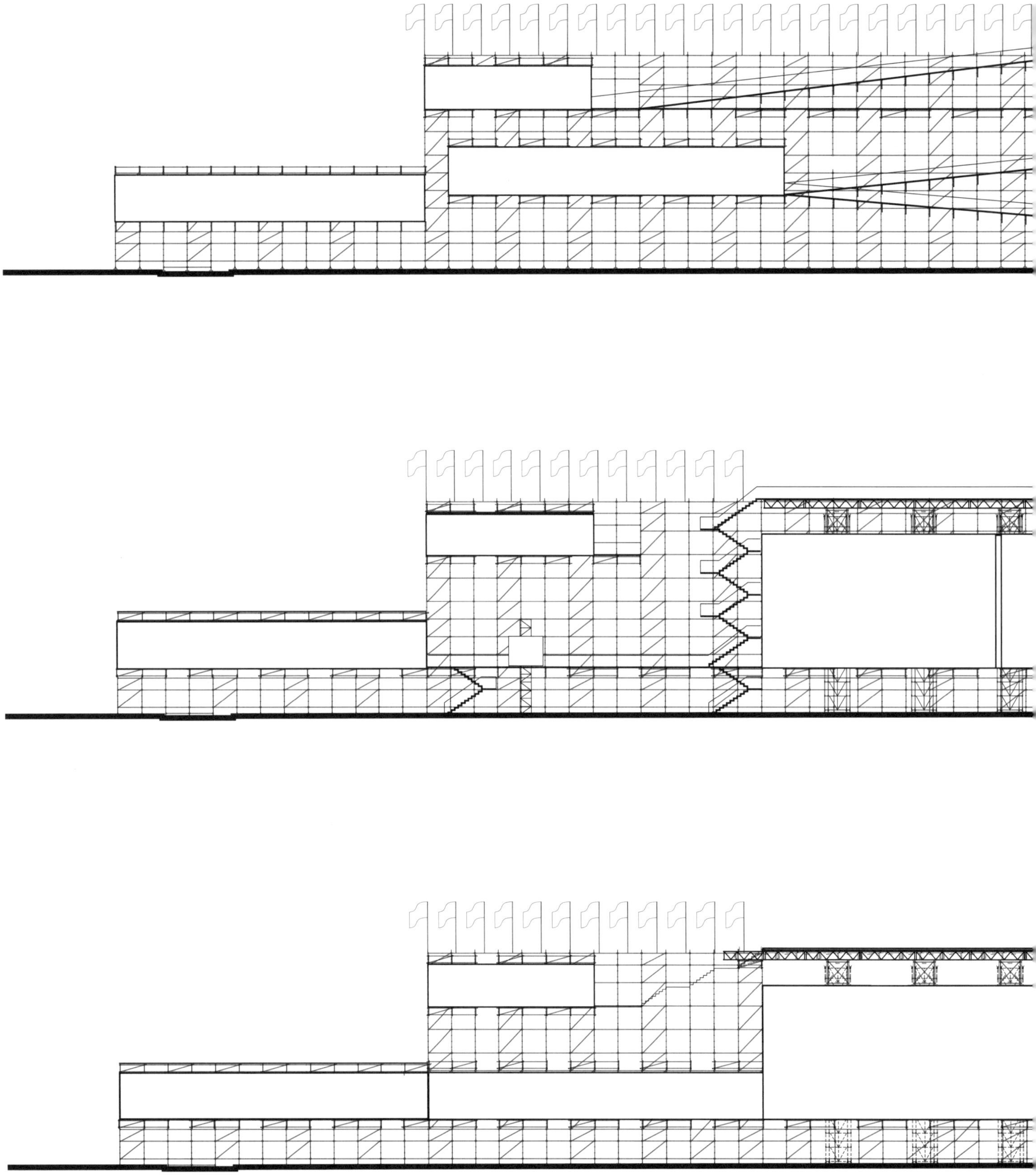

Longitudinal sections

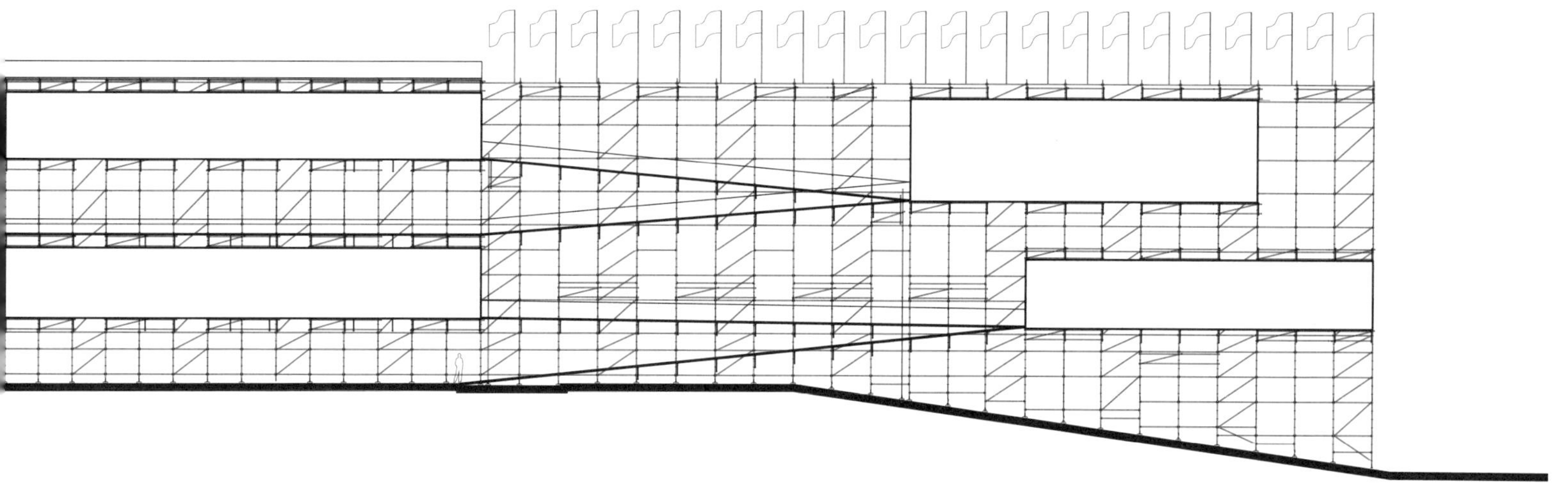

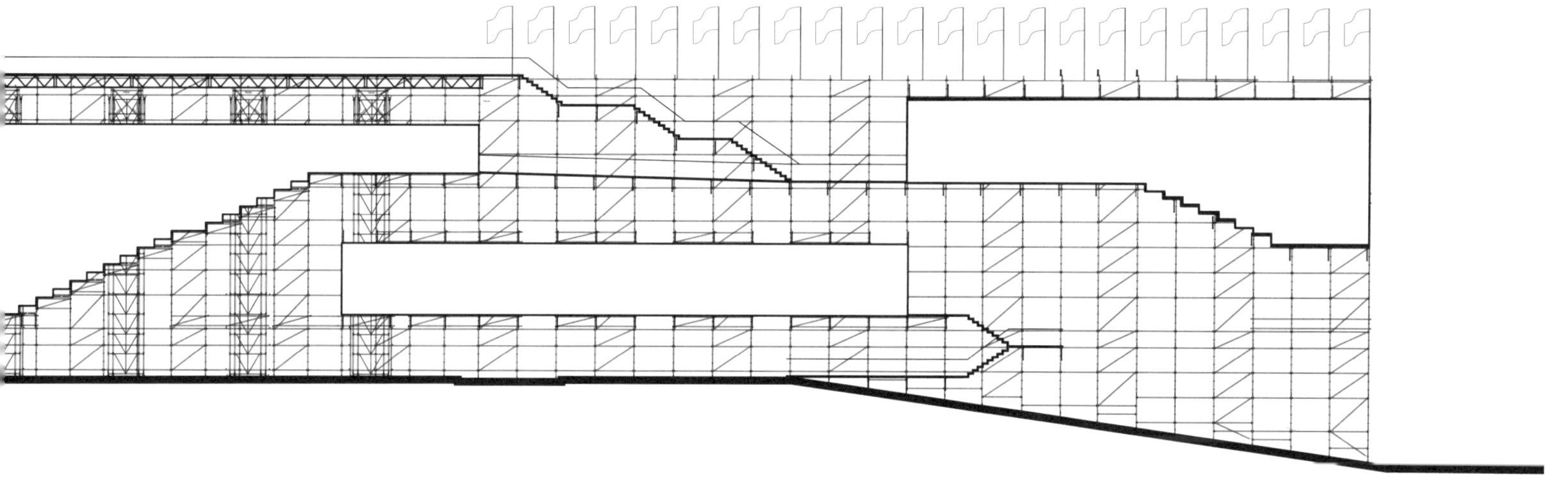

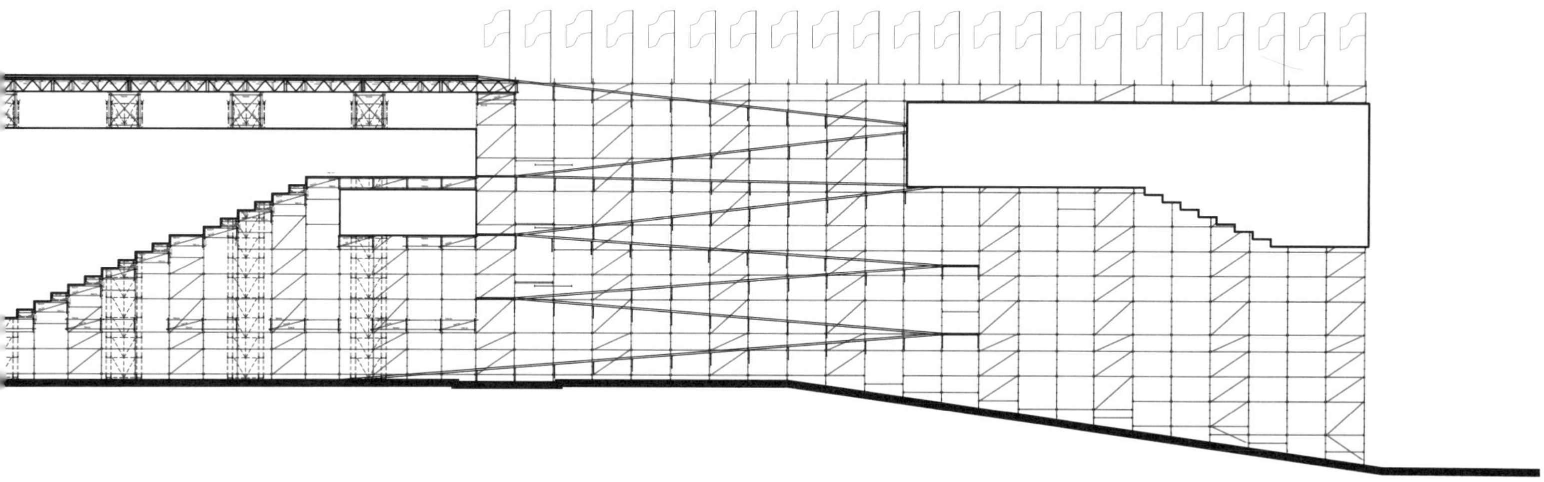

://HU
MANI
DADE
2012

LANGAGE
语言
LANGAGE
语言
ЯЗЫК
人类
人类
LENGUAJE
LANGUAGE
HUMANIDAD
ЯЗЫК
HUMANKIND
LANGAGE
человечество
HUMANIDAD
HUMANITE
语言
HUMANKIND
человечество

Santa Teresa House, Rio de Janeiro

2017

This house is parallel to the contour lines and totally adapted to the land, while also being invisible from the street. It sits on a slope in Santa Teresa, a hilly neighbourhood in central Rio de Janeiro, on a densely green area and across ten metres of uneven terrain. The upper floor is built near the street, facilitating construction and access.

The house has two floors: on the upper level is the entrance, kitchen, dining room and bedrooms, while the living room is on the lower level, two metres below. Given the slope, every permanent-use environment offers panoramic views. The two levels are connected by a glazed gallery, located in the part surrounded by the street. The roof, the most important element of the design, is composed of four different inclination lines and two different materials.

The house is not seen from the street, as if it were not there. It is built in a protected area of Rio de Janeiro, and all the trees must be preserved, which also guarantees the privacy of the residents: the opacity draws silhouettes, seen from both inside and outside. At night, artificial light changes the perception, and makes this part of the house look like a giant torch.

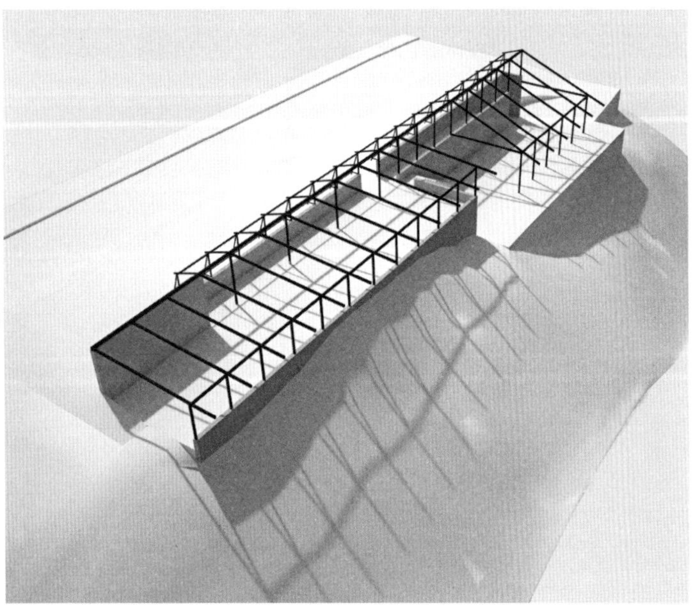

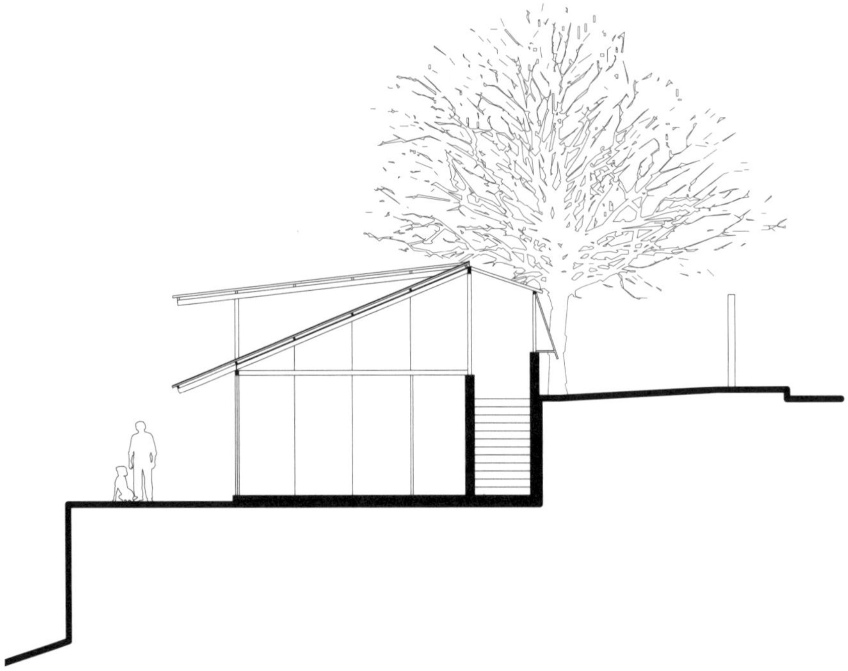

Cross-section

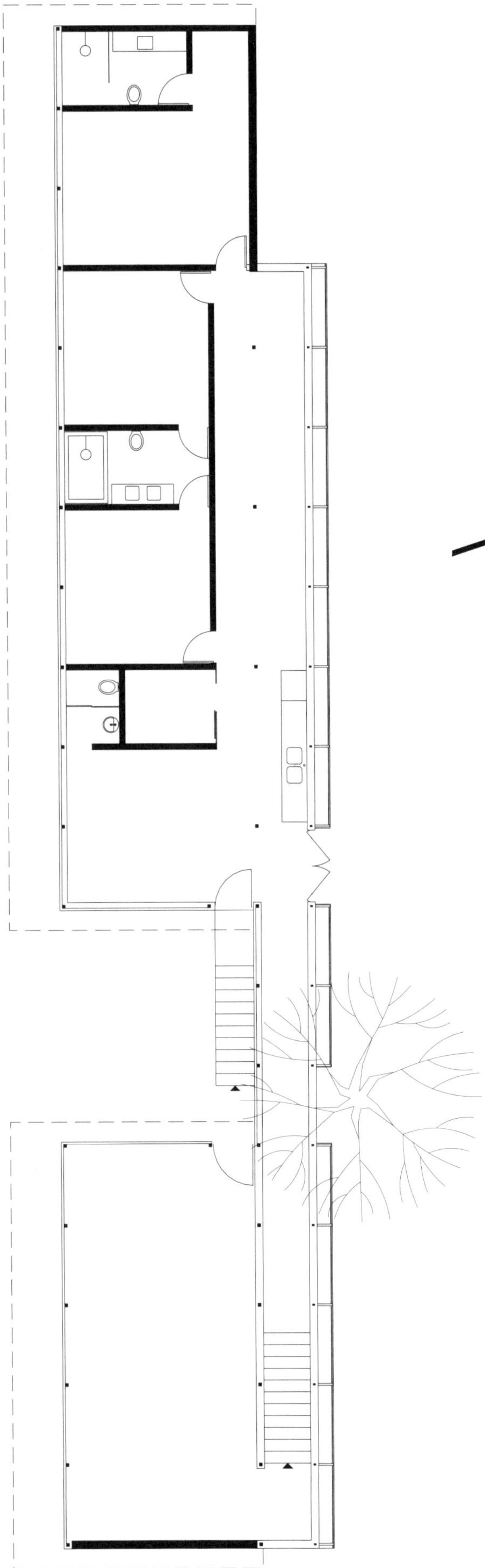

Ground floor

Vatican Chapel, Venice Architecture Biennale

2018

The Holy See took part in the Venice Architecture Biennale for the first time in 2018, the event's 16th edition. The theme of the Vatican chapel was proposed to ten architects, invited by the curator Francesco Dal Co: they were commissioned to build ten chapels within the densely wooded area at the end of the Island of San Giorgio Maggiore in Venice, which had never been opened to the public before. The project enhances the beauty of this place, briefly accentuating the space.

Four steel beams (12 × 12 × 800 cm) compose the ensemble: one part is a pew, and the other part is a cross, the two traditional elements of the Catholic church. They are built upon seven pieces of concrete (12 × 12 × 200 cm) which provides its metric.

The steel beams are made of highly polished stainless steel that reflects the surroundings: the chapel may even disappear at certain moments, and the ensemble's shadow sometimes stands out more than the object itself. The structure is completed by a natural dome among the trees.

The chapel is almost invisible. It is an ethereal project that speaks metaphorically of the passage of life, of existence and of non-existence.

The presence of history surrounds it, and the bench and cross give it a timeless quality.

Vatican Chapel, Venice Architecture Biennale

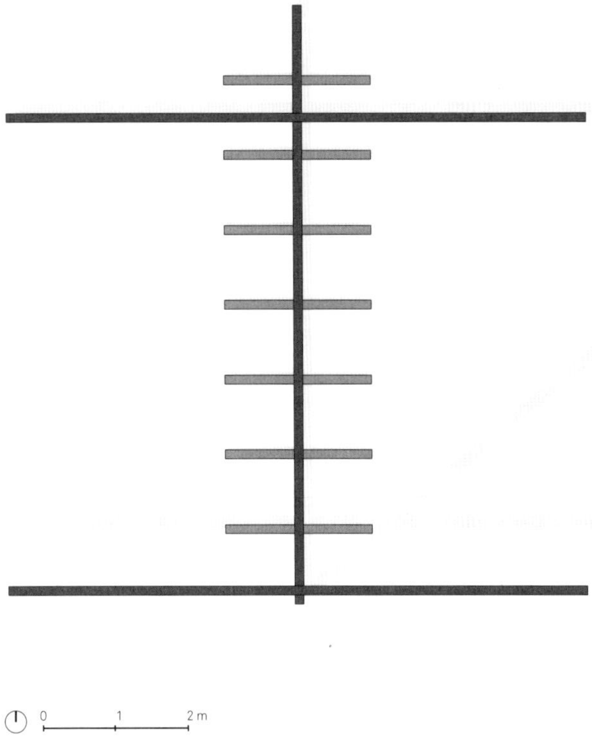
0
1
2 m

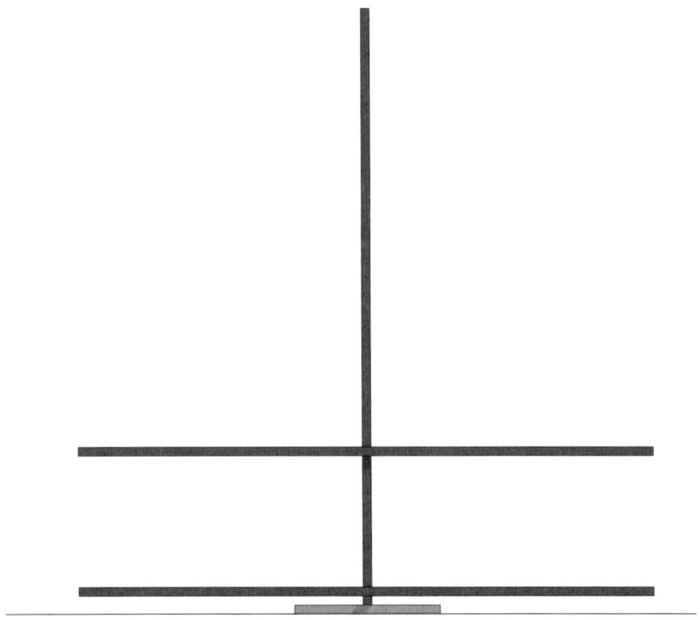

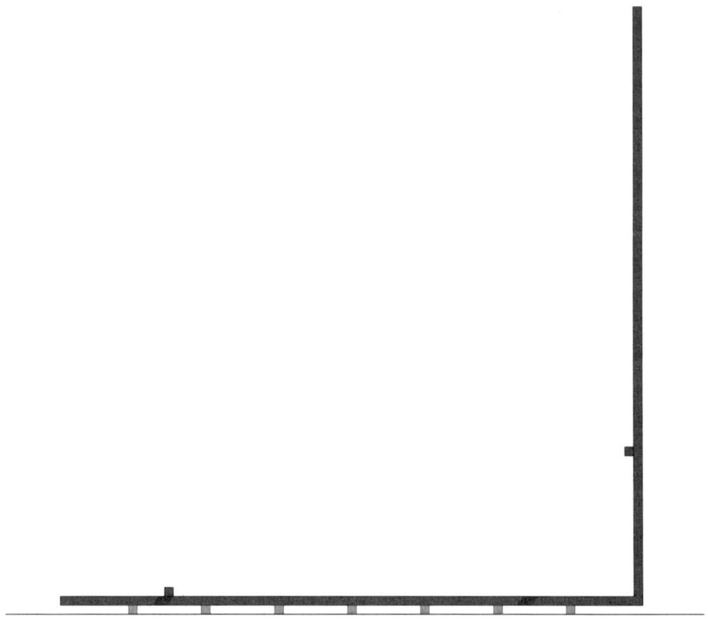

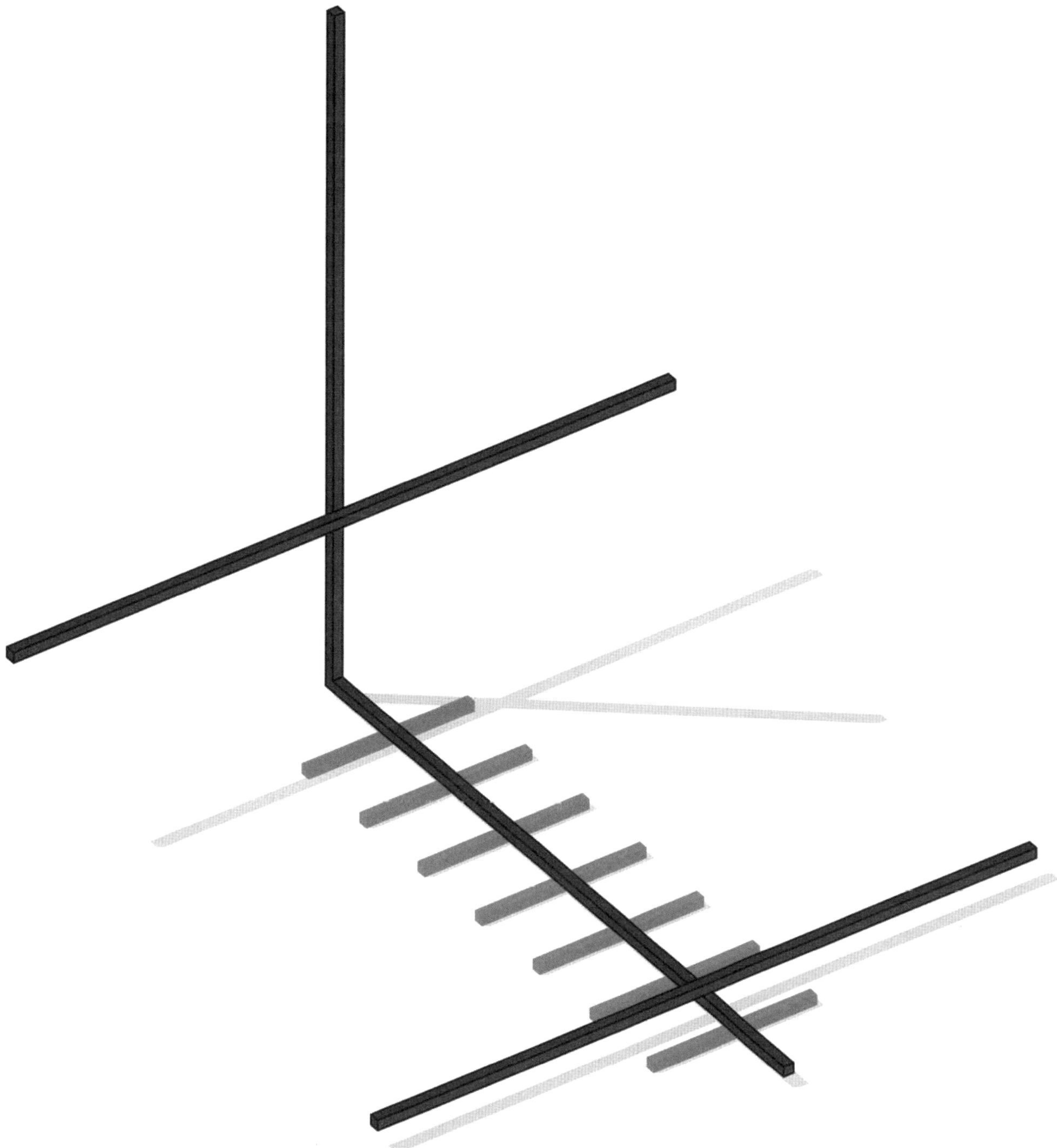

Vatican Chapel, Venice Architecture Biennale

Verdi House, Barcelona

Ballast, Venice Architecture Biennale

2018

A couple of benches, where people can sit and rest: this is an active response for the democratic space as proposed by Grafton Architects, the curators of the 2018 edition of the Venice Architecture Biennale, titled *Freespace*. The project was conceived after observing the context of the Biennale and the city of Venice: there is a need to pause and rest in the distant gardens of the Biennale.

Given the imagery of the city and its boats, the cables used for this installation are navy ropes, which used to be produced at the Corderie in the Arsenale. Furthermore, the immense blocks of concrete are a reference to the sea defences.

This object is also about the “active reality of the forces”, as sculptor Richard Serra put it. The opposition between the apparent lightness of the 32-metre-long navy ropes and the huge tension on these cables means that a heavy mass is required. Each bench is supported by two ensembles of concrete blocks, arranged differently upon each other. There is one only point of stability, with no connections in between.

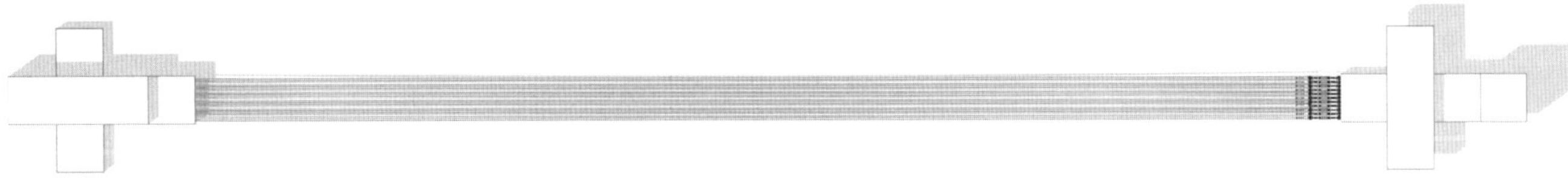

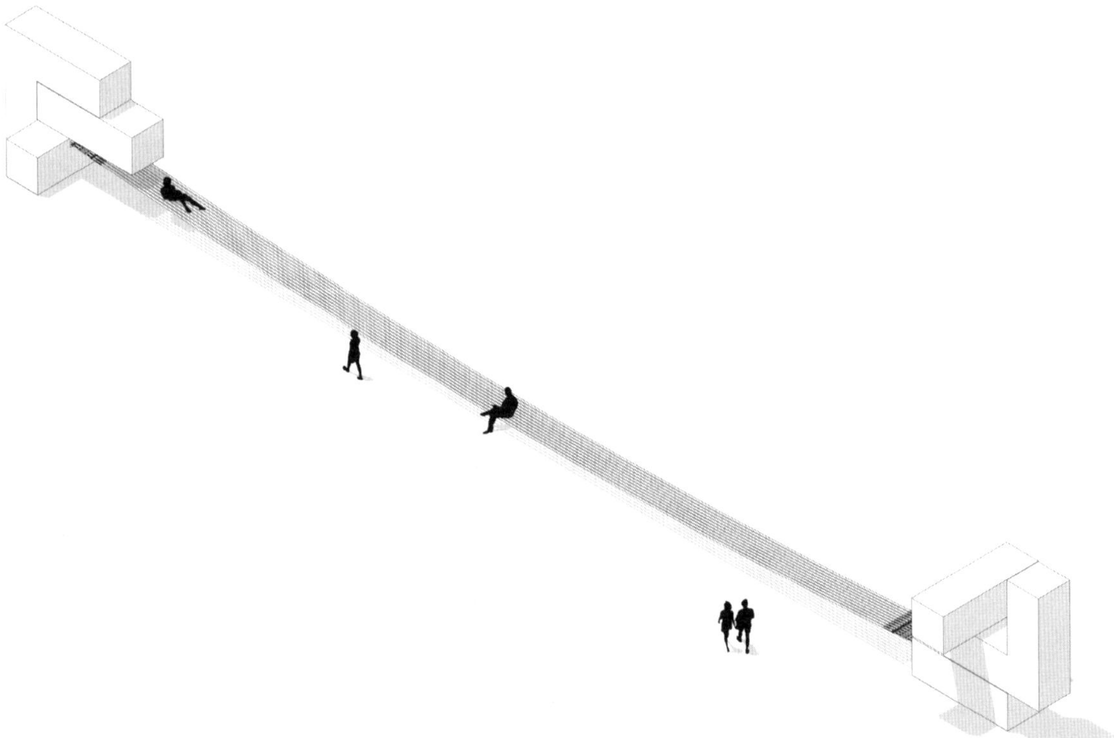

Ballast, Venice Architecture Biennale

Ballast, Venice Architecture Biennale

Ministry for All exhibition, New York
2019

Ministry for All paired Carla Juaçaba and artist Marcelo Cidade in an indirect collaboration. The project exposed the physical infrastructures of the gallery space at Storefront for Art and Architecture, in order to comment on the social and political foundations of the built environment. This site-specific installation, created entirely with Storefront's existing infrastructural elements, undressed the gallery's iconic façade to shed light on the theatricality and vulnerability of architecture. The project was made of two separate actions: firstly, Carla dismantled the iconic façade of the gallery, and unexpectedly revealed an imperfect and improvised construction beneath it. Secondly, Marcelo made an installation inside the gallery, recomposing all the removed parts of the façade and setting them to float within the space.

The installation is made with nothing; an action, and a composition.

OREFRONT FOR ART & ARCHITECTU
MINISTRY FOR ALL
PARA TODOS
09.21–12.14
2019
MARCELO CIDADE
CARLA JUAÇABA

Storefront for Art
and Architecture
97 KENMARE STREET NEW YORK NY 10012 TEL 212 431 5795
www.storefrontnews.org
GALLERY HOURS TUESDAY - SATURDAY 11AM - 6PM

&
ARCHITECTURE
MINISTRY
FOR
ALL
MINISTÉRIO
PARA
TODOS
09.21-
12.14
2019
CARLA
JUAÇABA
MARCELO
CIDADE

Ministry for All exhibition, New York

Videiras House, Rio de Janeiro

2022

Made from 60-centimetre clay blocks, this house is a line of clay on the landscape, protected from the North sun with openings onto the main view. The view happens between the openings, where some blocks are missing. The only balcony is in between the bedrooms, also behind the *cobogós* façade. The climate in the mountains of Rio de Janeiro is eight degrees Celsius lower than in the city, so the house is exposed to the sun all day long. The glass-projected eaves allow the sun to warm up the house, while also protecting the dwelling from the intense rains.

Videiras House, Rio de Janeiro

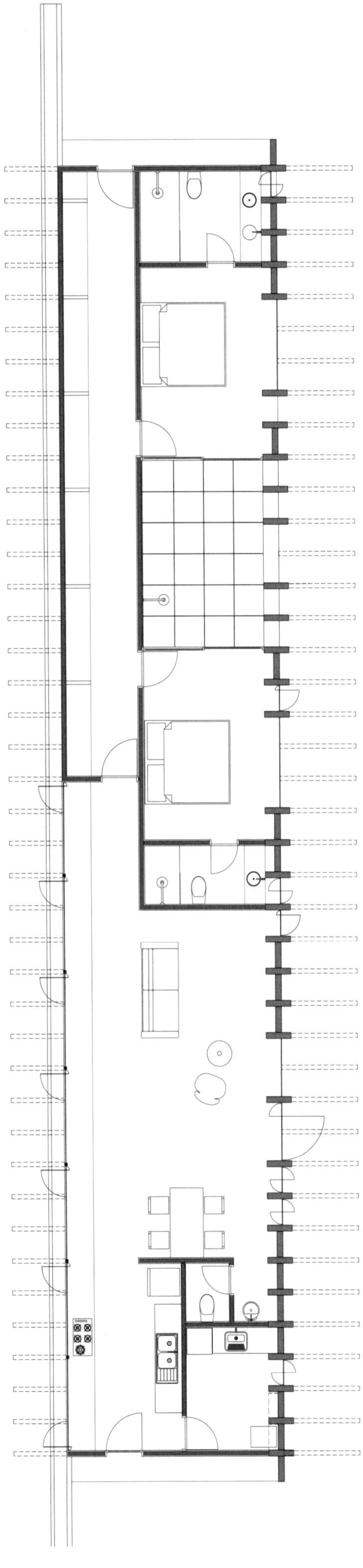

Ground floor

Videiras House, Rio de Janeiro

Videiras House, Rio de Janeiro

Videiras House, Rio de Janeiro

Pedra do Tempo, Lisbon

2022

The exhibition *First Stone* presents 74 original works in Portuguese stone, designed by 36 authors from fifteen countries. *Pedra do tempo* is a large-scale installation made out of black Foz Côa schist. It is composed of four solid pieces of stone, two laid on the floor as a base, and two standing, sculpted from the inside. Granulated sand dust passes through the elevated stones, just once, transforming the installation into an ephemeral performance: it is a kind of hourglass, speaking of a time that has already passed, of resources that have been exhausted. It is a statement about the fragility of natural ecosystems and the depletion of their resources over time, as further reflected by the fragility of this type of stone itself: it is easily chipped and broken, unlike other harder and more compact ones, like granite or marble.

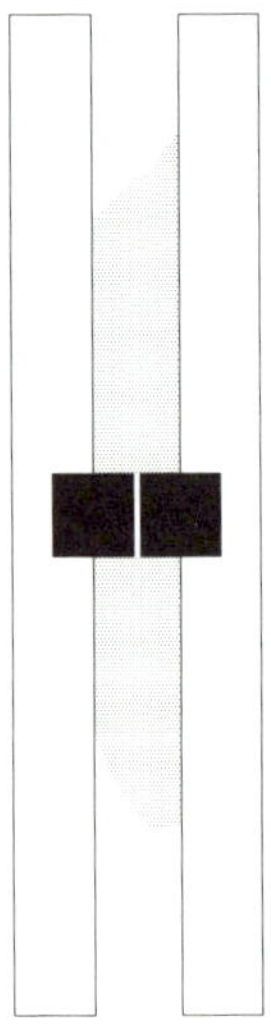

Pedra do Tempo, Lisbon

Fil d'air, Geneva

2022

Golden lines connect earth to trees. They are made by several brass lines, resting on a string. There is little desire to build, but rather to suggest a path to the darkest part of the trees. The difference in level of the existing ground gave a curve of five metres in height, where one passes through. It is a form of architecture, or a sketch of a project that wants to connect the terrain to the trees, infinitely. But only just touching the ground with its lightest weight.

This installation was carried out in the context of Open House Geneva.

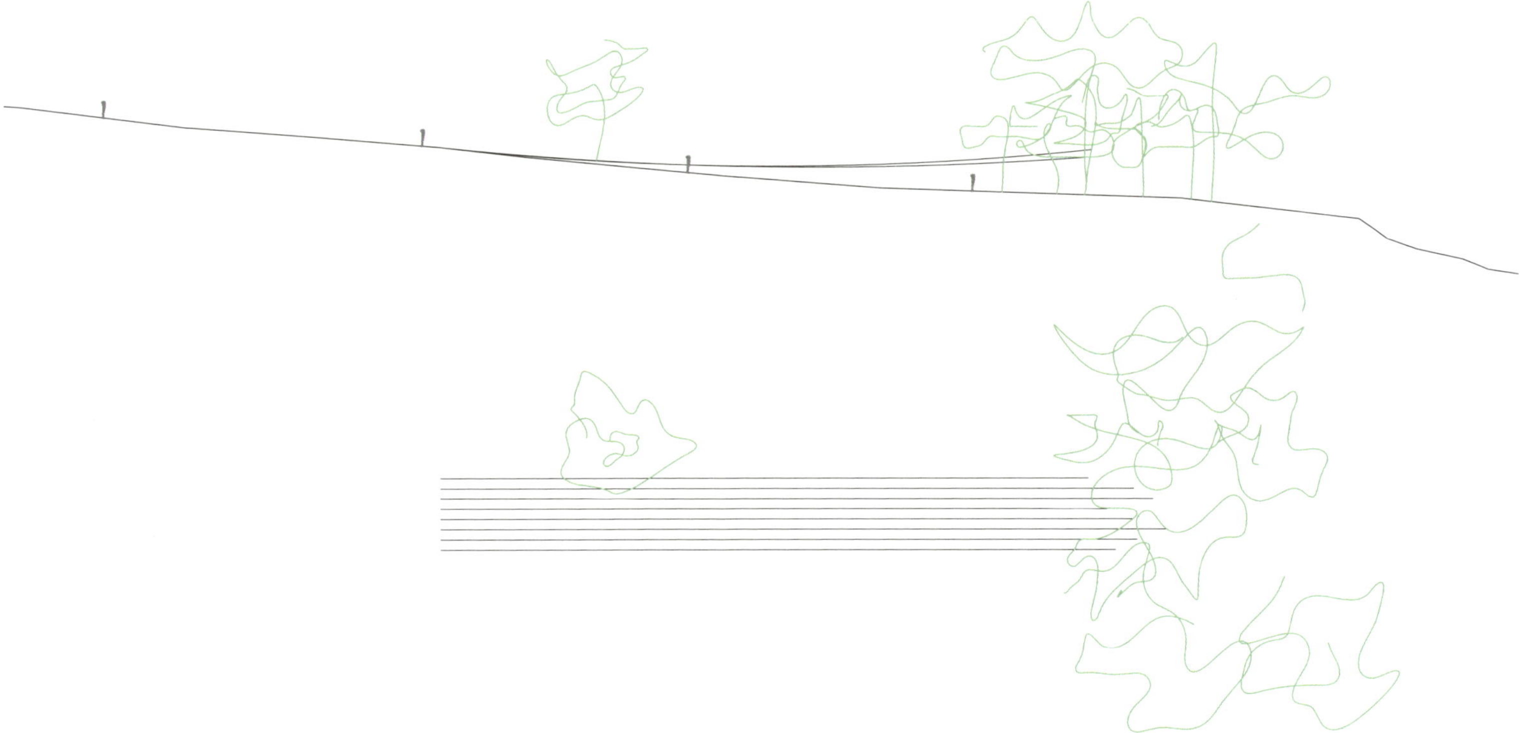

Fil d'air, Geneva

Flor de Café, Nepomuceno

2023-

Flor de Café is a movement that brings together over fifty local farmers in Nepomuceno (Minas Gerais), southeast Brazil. This new museum project aims to tell a different history of coffee, in an attempt to break with the extractivist coffee culture that took hold in the region in the late-18th century. This culture still prevails today, in what is considered to be one of the most important coffee-producing regions in Brazil.

The building is located on a plateau for coffee bean drying on the Vista Alegre estate, at an altitude of 1,100 metres. It is integrated into the landscape and in the open air, with views of mountain ranges and almost too much sky. The building includes a space for vocational training courses, in which workers learn the necessary skills to work in the entire coffee chain, i.e. to become baristas, master roasters, pickers, master driers and other such roles. There is also a cafeteria and, later on, there will be a restaurant and a hotel. The project will be built with roadside billboard modules, which are made from eucalyptus logs and sheet metal, for a simple and cheap construction. As and when a higher level of comfort is required, some programmes will have more density, or layers of thermal insulation (such as in the classrooms and coffee tasting rooms).

The project occupies the territory in an informal and ephemeral way. It takes its inspiration from the constructions of the Landless Workers' Movement (MST), the most important agrarian-social movement in Brazil today, which stands up for the rights of rural women and men.

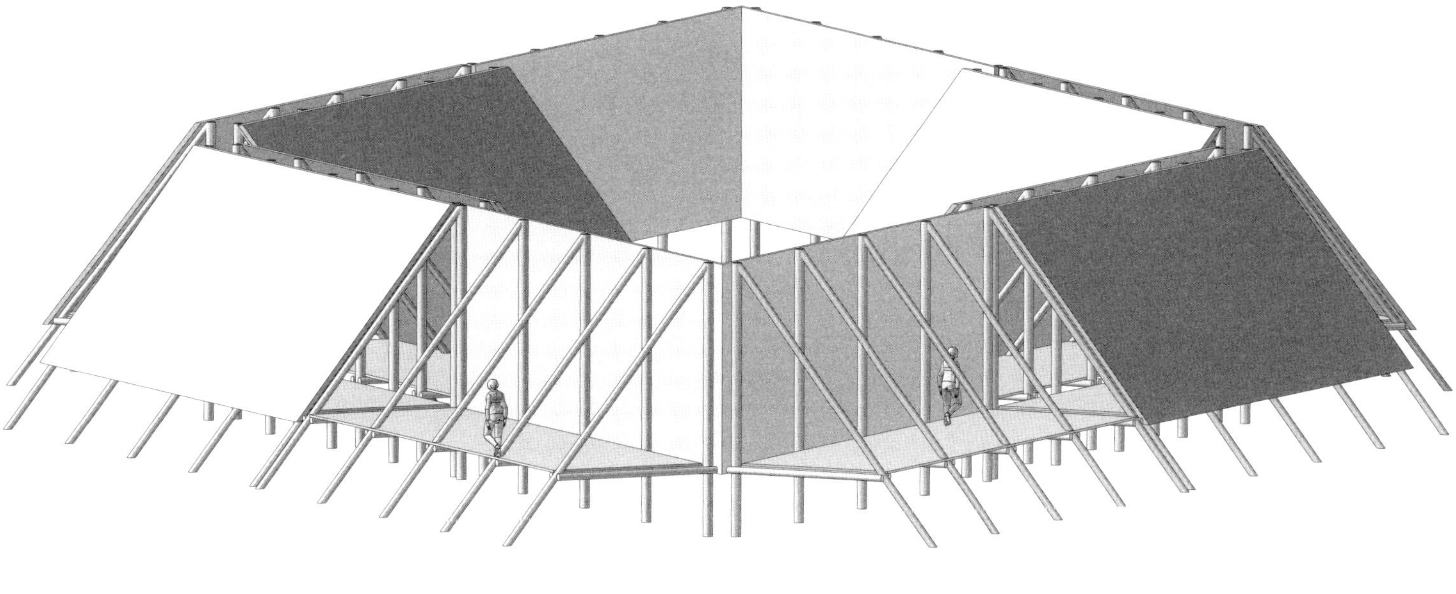

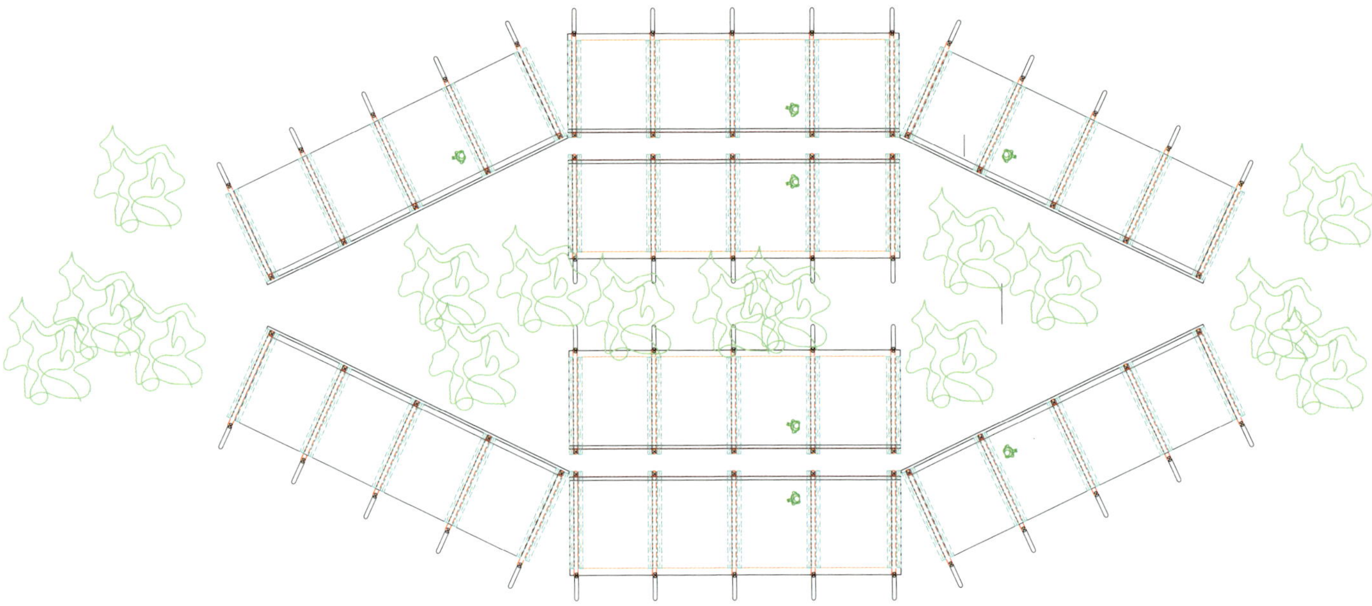

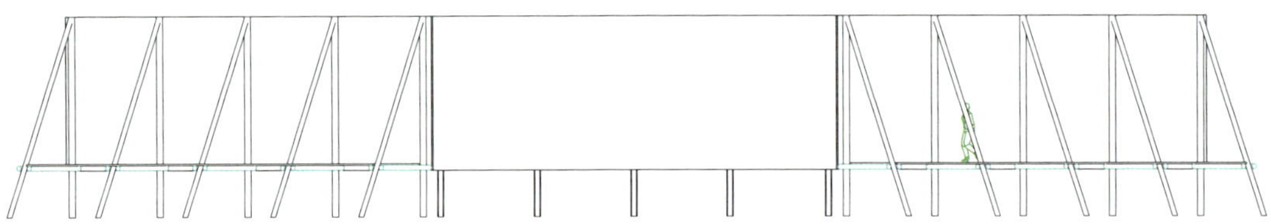

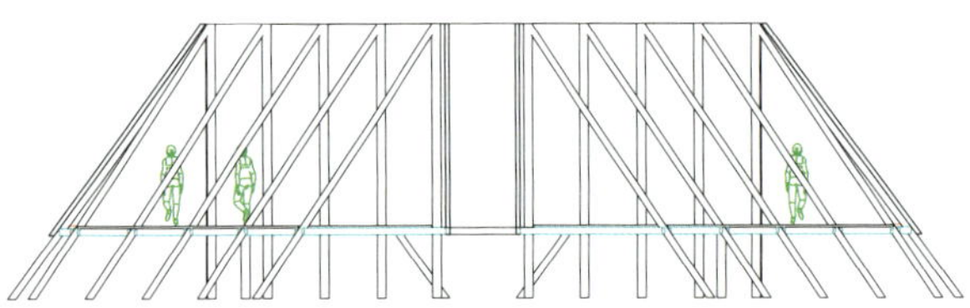

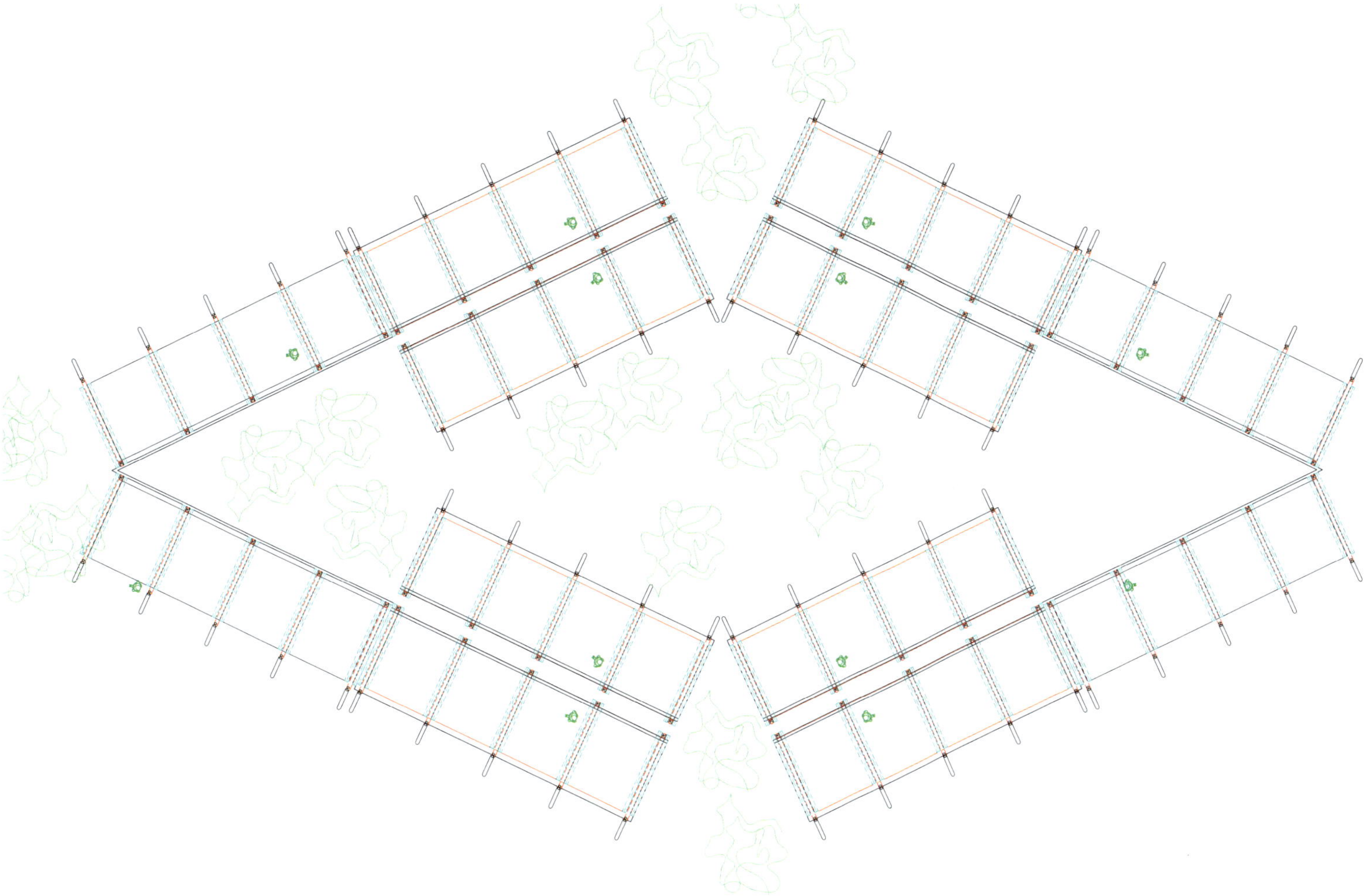

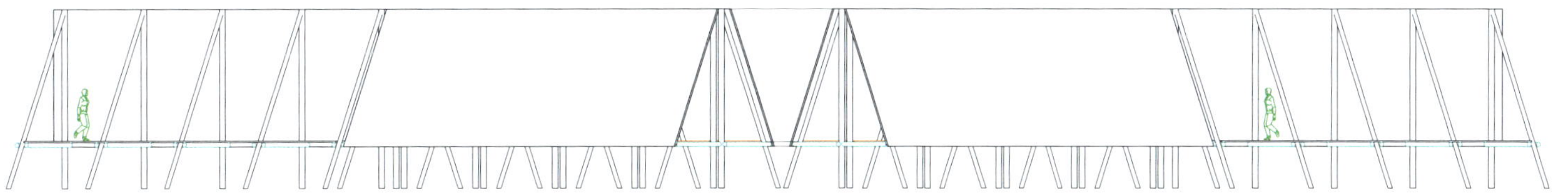

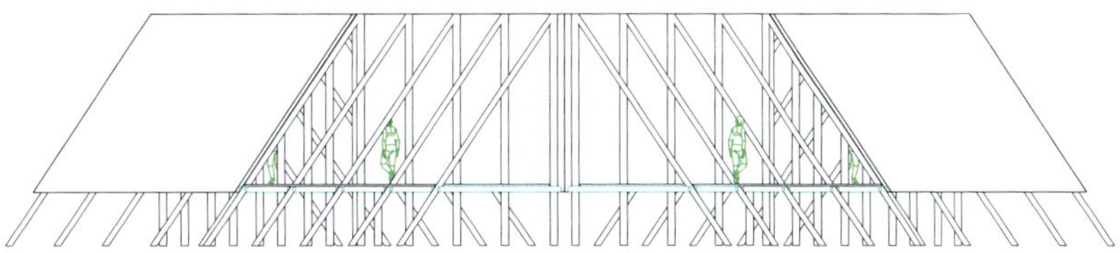

Credits

House-atelier, Itanhangá

Location Itanhangá, Brazil
Architects Carla Juaçaba, Mario Fraga
Design and construction years 2000-01
Photographs Fran Parente

House in Rio Bonito

Location Lumiar (Rio de Janeiro), Brazil
Architect Carla Juaçaba
Design and construction years 2004-05
Builder Max Engenharia
Photographs Nelson Kohn

Varanda House, Rio de Janeiro

Location Rio de Janeiro, Brazil
Architect Carla Juaçaba
Design and construction years 2007-08
Collaborators Joana Ramalhete, Nina Lucena
Structural engineer Pirajá dos Anjos
Metal structure construction D'Angeli Serviços de Engenharia
Building services Simon Merheb
Lighting Joana Marcier
Photographs Fran Parente

Isostasy, Mexico City

Location LIGA. Espacio para Arquitectura, Mexico City, Mexico
Architect Carla Juaçaba
Design and construction year 2012
Coordination Maki Leos
Graphic design Barbara Cutlak
Photographs Ramiro Chaves

Humanidade Pavilion, Rio de Janeiro

Location Rio de Janeiro, Brazil
Architect Carla Juaçaba
General coordination and exhibition design Bia Lessa
Design and construction year 2012
Collaborators Antonio Pedro Coutinho, Sergio García-Gasco Lominchar, Elza Burgos de la Prida and Pedro Varella (architects); Daniel Cuchicho, Rita D'Aguilar, Barbara Cutlak and Álvaro Pitas (students)
Light designer Paulo Pederneiras
Scenography direction Abel Gomes
Builder P&G Cenografia
Executive production Lucas Arruda
Structure MVD
Sound designer Dany Roland
Graphic design Cubículo
Landscape design Daniela Infante
Lighting Naldo Bueno
General coordination SRCOM
Content, curatorship FIESP/FIRJAN
Photographs Celso Brando, Leonardo Finotti

Santa Teresa House, Rio de Janeiro

Location Santa Teresa, Rio de Janeiro, Brazil
Architect Carla Juaçaba
Design and construction year 2017
Collaborator Carlos Saul Zebulun
Engineer CERNE enghenaria
Photographs Clovis Cunha, Federico Cairoli

Vatican Chapel, Venice Architecture Biennale

Location Island of San Giorgio Maggiore, Venice, Italy
Architect Carla Juaçaba
Design and construction year 2018
Architect collaborator Clovis Cunha
Consultant engineer CERNE Engenharia (Geraldo Filizola, Arthur Menezes)
Consultant manager TTE -Tecno Brevetti Team/Luigi Cocco
Builder Secco Sistemi
Photographs Federico Cairoli

Ballast, Venice Architecture Biennale

Location Venice, Italy
Architect Carla Juaçaba
Design and construction year 2018
Architect collaborator Clovis Cunha
Consultant engineer CERNE Engenharia (Geraldo Filizola, Arthur Menezes)
Builder Babau Bureau
Photographs Federico Cairoli

Ministry for All exhibition, New York

Location Storefront for Art and Architecture, New York, USA
Authors Carla Juaçaba (architect), Marcelo Cidade (artist)
Design and construction year 2019
Curator José Esparza Chong
Graphic design estúdio campo
Photographs Nei Valente

Videiras House, Rio de Janeiro

Location Rio de Janeiro, Brazil
Architect Carla Juaçaba
Builder Gregorio Rosenbush
Light design Clovis Cunha
Design and construction year 2022
Photographs Pedro Kok

Pedra do Tempo, Lisbon

Location Museu Nacional dos Coches, Lisbon, Portugal
Architect Carla Juaçaba
Design and construction year 2022
Curator Guta Moura Guedes
Stone supplier and production Solicel
Photographs Ricardo Gonçalves

Fil d'air, Geneva

Location Geneva, Switzerland
Architect Carla Juaçaba
Design and construction year 2022
Photographs Julien Gremaud

Flor de Café, Nepomuceno

Location Nepomuceno (Minas Gerais), Brazil
Architect Carla Juaçaba
Design and construction years 2023-
Client Flor de Café
Project founder Milena Rodrigues

NEXUS

A conversation between Eduardo Souto de Moura and Carla Juaçaba

The Open Space

Exhibition Design

Carla Juaçaba

Carla Juaçaba When I was a student, I was enchanted by Peter Brook's theatre, with its imperfection and impermanence. He uses so few elements to communicate his theatre —but it has nothing to do with minimalism! It has to do with an economy of means, of language, and it's very poetic, very symbolic, and loaded with meaning. And I said to myself back then: one day, if I ever do architecture, I want to do it like Peter Brook does theatre, using hardly anything.

I find it very curious that the only art you can never see again is theatre. It's the most ephemeral art of all: it ends the moment it's finished. You can try to get closer to its language through books and images, but it's impossible.

Jerzy Grotowski invented "poor theatre" in the 1960s in Poland, whereby he said: I don't need anything —no light, no clothes, no text, only the spectator. But he never said: I don't need any stage design, or scenery. The physical theatrical space is the only thing we can grasp, nothing else.

Carla Juaçaba and Eduardo Souto de Moura in Porto.

The space for this kind of theatre is usually a concentrated space, only ever with a few people: it looks like an operating theatre of old, where spectators would watch the surgery.

Then the Italians appropriated the concept using *arte povera*, but I think it was much less essential, and they didn't quite get there.

Eduardo Souto de Moura I don't like theatre; theatre in Portugal is so declamatory, so boring...

CJ I used to hate theatre too, but there's something so essential about Brook and Grotowski. I learned so much from them, and I was able to look at our discipline through the lens of another one. I think it's a good language exercise.

Peter Brook wrote many books, with the intention of recording all his theatrical language, which I don't think is possible. But if you read his work at length, you can get a good sense of what he wanted to communicate. There is one particular thing he said, which I find the most beautiful of all: "Nothing is entirely given... you need your imagination to continue."

ESDM Álvaro Siza once designed a ballet set that had a light on the ceiling, and that was it.

CJ How beautiful!

ESDM It completes the image. When I saw Siza's chapel, I really liked it. In fact, it was the only one I liked. And I asked myself... where does it come from? Now I'm beginning to get it, to understand it even better.

CJ And if we talk about impermanence, for example, we might refer to things that were never built, like Cedric Price's Fun Palace, or things that no longer exist, like Aldo Rossi's Teatro del Mondo. It is such strong architecture; even something that never existed can still be part of our cultural world. Architecture is permanent in any case! Even if it's gone or never existed.

There's another beautiful quote from Peter Brook: "Is the empty space insufficient? If the answer is yes, then one starts to consider what the indispensable elements are." But this has nothing to do with the theatre of that American minimalist, Bob Wilson, which is very graphic. I'm not interested in anything graphic, not even in architecture.

ESDM There was a reaction to postmodernism: minimalism emerged in opposition to it. At that moment, I look at minimalist things and I don't see a movement of depuration; I see laziness, rather than a search for something. And then there's a difference between those who work hard to achieve things and those who don't work at all and contribute nothing.

And in architecture, you have a moment when you put cement on the floor, paint it white, bring out a pair of shoes —and there you have a shop. So, right now, I'm a bit annoyed by the minimalists.

CJ For the Vatican chapels for the 2018 Venice Architecture Biennale, the curator Francesco Dal Co sent a video to all the participants. I was unable to visit the island of San Giorgio Maggiore, but I settled on an idea for the project after I saw that video: it showed the light of Venice pulsating, a metaphor for life, behind a centuries-old garden, where you could make out an ancient city beyond it all. And that was it! I thought a curator sending a video like that showed a great level of abstraction and beauty, and I felt I had to respond to that level of abstraction.

ESDM When I see your wall-less chapel, I feel that there is no need for walls because the walls are already there... the trees are the walls.

CJ That's right —like Peter Brook's theatre, you can sit in the chapel and imagine a dome among the trees, if you like, and be in communion with nature. It's a pity that the word "communion" is only used in a religious sense, or perhaps it is just a religious thing, in the wider sense.

ESDM Architecture has to be in communion with and overlap with nature. It is different to nature, so it has to be autonomous. It has to go against the rules of nature. But it exists in contradiction to it, because otherwise it becomes naturalistic and loveable.

CJ In my presentations I always show the two chapels, mine and yours, and that's not just because I love you. It's because I think it's so beautiful that the lightest chapel of all was placed next to the heaviest one.

ESDM I chose that place; I didn't know where your work would go.

CJ But it was Francesco Dal Co who then put me next to you.

ESDM I really like the contrast.

CJ I think it's a cultural question of the relationship between Portuguese architecture and the ground, which is always deep-rooted and topographic. Professor Ana Luiza Nobre's research into the ground makes this very clear. And Brazilian architecture, as Portugal's Alexandre Alves Costa has said, is "a horizontal line raised from the ground".

Once, when I was talking to Kenneth Frampton, he asked why there was this obsession in Brazil with long-span buildings, that require a kind of technology that "only you [in Brazil] know how to do". In Ana Luiza Nobre's research, this becomes clear when she says that in Brazilian architecture the floor is a public and democratic space for meeting: consider the space of the Art Museum of São Paulo (MASP) by Lina Bo Bardi, or the Faculty of Architecture at the University of São Paulo (FAUSP) by João Batista Vilanova Artigas. And only afterwards comes the desire for technique to achieve this. This doesn't come first, there is no obsession with technique; first comes the desire for a democratic ground space that can sustain all of this.

ESDM I think the Modern Movement was made for Latin America. Marxism was made in negatives. And, in the end, it only materialised in hot countries, like Cuba, Venezuela and Brazil.

The Modern Movement was born in Russia, the Soviet avant-garde, the Netherlands and Germany; France had one case, Le Corbusier, but that's not a movement. The only place where it was completely based on the design of architecture and urbanism was Brazil. I've only seen this in Brasília, when I go into the blocks, and I see the pilotis and those gardens that go inside the buildings and houses. It's so beautiful, when you have the doors open and everything. So Le Corbusier's dream, of the exterior coming into the interior, has been achieved in Brazil.

CJ And it's still happening now!

ESDM Is there no postmodernism going on?

CJ Very little, but there is a mannerism, like in some recent works in Brasília, that I don't like, with the "long span" all out of proportion and with no purpose. But I also find it very difficult to work on the scale of Brasília.

ESDM But, curiously enough, the projects themselves are not very large in Brazil. There's a discrepancy in Brazil between Lúcio Costa's grandiose plan and the final projects. Oscar Niemeyer's works are not big: the cathedral is small, almost domestic.

CJ It's true that the ministries are not large, but their esplanade is immense, and huge protests there always seem tiny.

ESDM I think the scale of the plan's architecture is out of step. The quality of Niemeyer's work is wonderful—he's perhaps the architect that I like the most—but the design of the city has certain proportions, as in the avenues, the monumental part, whereby even the cathedral is small.

I was explaining that Portuguese architects have never done anything big. They're always small. They only have a small territory to work on, between the sea and Spain. And maybe that notion was carried over to Brazil.

CJ Let's go back to the ground, and what I wanted to say about the two chapels at the Venice Biennale. Our first action on the territory is to modify the ground, the foundations as a first drawing, a drawing that is felt from the ground: the drawing is the ground, and the ground is the drawing. If we think about Norman Foster's chapel, it's the opposite in that sense: it has a steel platform floating on the ground, the relationship with the ground is different.

The seven foundation pieces of my chapel are twelve centimetres from the ground, everything is twelve centimetres. The foundation, the pieces of the cross, add up to a bench.

ESDM Why twelve centimetres?

CJ It was the measurement the design gave me. I just don't like it when I hear people saying that it's not architecture, that it's a sculpture, an installation. I don't think so!

ESDM No! Nobody sits on a sculpture!

CJ And I am reminded of a phrase that I love, by Aldo Rossi. He says, more or less: "Theatre is very similar to architecture: something will happen!". The chapel has a programme, a purpose; you go there, sit on the pews, and look at the cross that represents suffering, it is the synthesis of a programme. I keep having to explain that this chapel is architecture, even though it doesn't have a roof, or walls...

ESDM The walls are already there. Francesco Dal Co chose those two trees in the background, and located his chapel. And it's all green anyway, so the walls were already there. The architect of Malaparte House in Capri, Adalberto Libera, said: "I arrived and the house was already there, I just drew the landscape." How wonderful!

CJ Changing the subject, I remember a conversation I had with your engineer, Rui Furtado, about the Braga stadium. He told me about and showed me the pieces of architectural engineering that were not necessary, but were still there, and I was so shocked. Why did you do that? It was a staircase that was not actually a staircase.

ESDM It was part of a staircase-void composition, so I still put a staircase there, but left it unused.

One thing I like about architects is the urge to create unused elements; the floating staircase has such fine, thin proportions that it couldn't exist as a staircase. Like the wing of an aeroplane: when you go up the steps, the wing looks so thin. Do you know how thick the part of the wing that goes into the plane is? A metre! But because it is rounded and tapered it looks really thin.

CJ I brought up this topic because when I made the chapel I had seven concrete pieces, but technically it only needed three. Then I remembered the Braga stadium and put in all seven, because I thought that a certain rhythm was necessary. The space is so empty, it was like it needed a unit of measurement, a metric.

Another important thing about the chapel was my discussion with Francesco Dal Co about the structural reinforcements of the pews and the cross, and also about welding. They didn't want it to be welded because the chapel was going to be dismantled. But I said: "Here we have to weld, then we can work out what to do." And the welding was perfect and beautiful, done by a craftsman, so, in the end, Dal Co was very proud to show it. And the cross was funny: Dal Co asked me to "raise" it, in case people tried to hang from it.

ESDM That welding story is so beautiful. There's another story about a very beautiful weld: Mies van der Rohe's Barcelona chair. The chair stands up because of the weld. There's a book that tells the story of this contradiction: the design itself is simple and cheap, but the weld takes two days to complete. It has these "triangles" that you've probably never noticed.

CJ I'm going to show you that *Isostasy* object that floats in space.

ESDM I tried to copy it! I wanted to do an installation that I'd been asked to do: it was a box that had a floating plate held up by magnetic forces, but it couldn't find a static position, that was the problem. It didn't work.

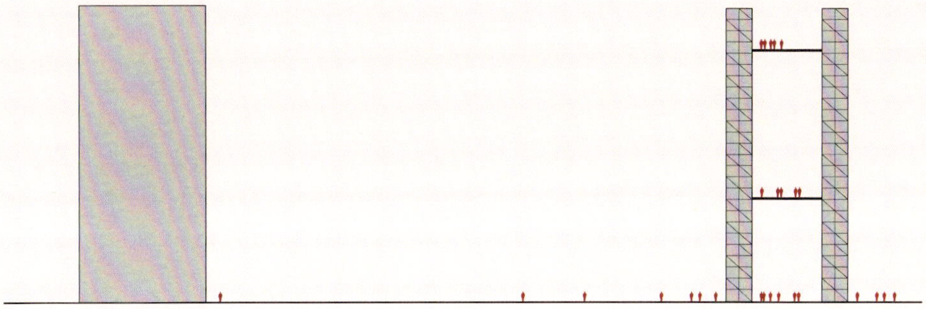

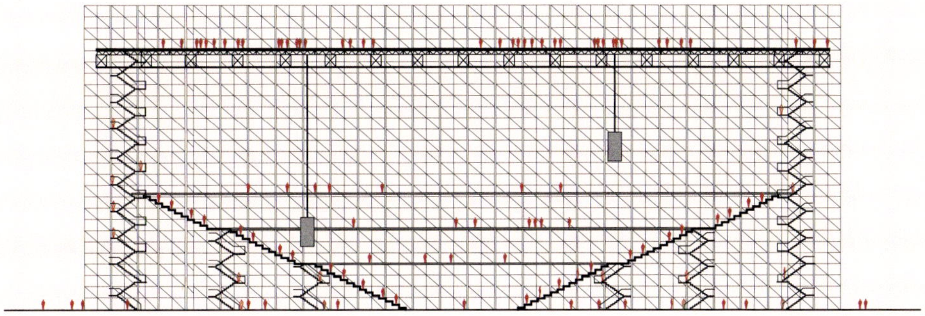

Ministry for All (2020) is an imaginary building for Brasília. A utopic project, set among the grandiose structures of the city's Esplanade of Ministries: the idea is that another ministry would be built next to the cathedral, with the same dimensions as the other ministries and at the same distance from them. However, this one would be made from scaffolding, as a temporary building. It could be a place for public debate, where one could follow the activities of a potential monument to democracy.

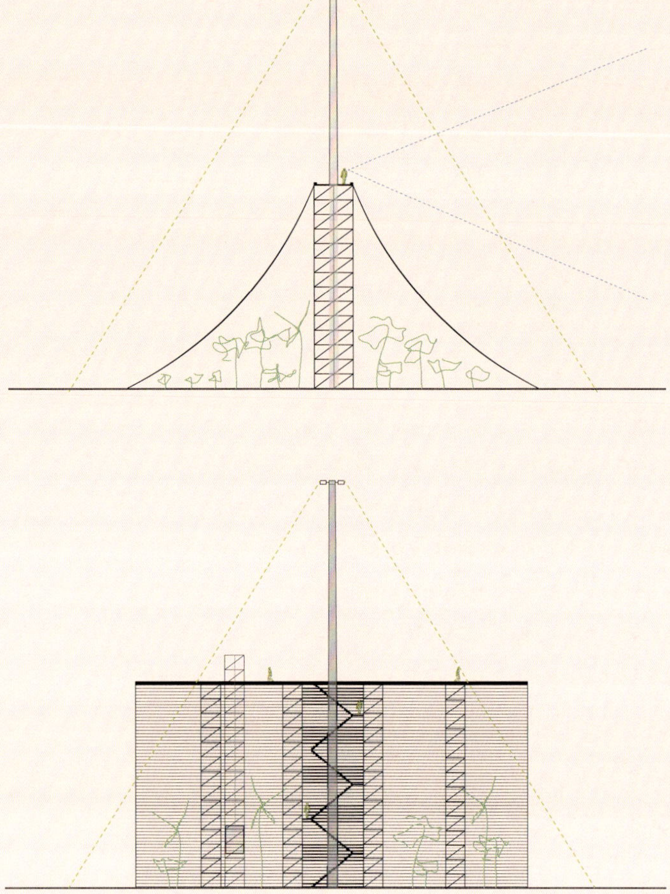

Burle Marx Plant Nursery, Flamengo Park, Rio de Janeiro, 2020

To make that positive and negative power you need an absurd amount of force. My installation kept moving and sliding. And so, I thought: I'll copy Carla. That idea is ingenious!

CJ What made the whole assemblage stable was a rubber washer. It took me a week to figure out that this would solve the slippage problem. You know what happened next: with the earthquake, everything fell over and broke anyway!

I called a physicist to do a statics-magnetism equation. The result came in after the piece was finished, and it said to leave five centimetres between the magnets. At the end he wrote: "The result may not agree with reality." But it was completely right.

ESDM This is a beautiful story. And what happened to the installation is so beautiful. There's a story in the bible that ends like this: "And you shall be dust...". It relates to the chapel. They are closely connected, these two things.

CJ My installation in Geneva, *Fil d'air* (2022), connects the earth to the trees, and I think it is a way to enter into the shade of the trees. It uses the same thickness of brass as in the *Isostasy* piece. I had a friend who went there to see it and couldn't actually find the piece, it was so invisible.

Changing the subject again, I never showed you the Ministry for All. Now that Lula da Silva has won the presidential elections, it may no longer be a utopian object. Like a ready-made, the idea would be to build another ministry, with the same measurements and distance between them, but made of scaffolding. Temporary, though without a fixed timeframe —the four years of Lula's presidency, say. And it would be a monument to democracy, an agora where you can enter from all sides, with two symmetrical stands, and the stage is the ground of Brasília.

The project arose from a question posed by the curator Hans Ulrich Obrist: what would you do with the Flamengo Embankment, designed by Roberto Burle Marx, and with Oscar Niemeyer's Serpentine Gallery pavilion, that would be rebuilt on the embankment temporarily?

After a few days, I answered: I would carry out Burle Marx's unrealised dream. I'd create a plant nursery, but also a suspended public space, a belvedere, so that everyone could look down and see his drawings on the ground.

ESDM That idea brings together those other three works of yours: the chapel, the tree park and the scaffolding.

In 1970, the English theatre director Peter Brook (1925-2022) started experimenting, on the floor, with his "carpet shows": there was no need for a ceiling to hang anything from, no need for a raised stage. With just a few objects or words, he was able to evoke an image.

By returning to the most primitive theatrical action, i.e. street performance, Peter Brook continually asked himself what a theatre should look like: "Is the empty space insufficient? If the answer is yes, then one starts to consider what the indispensable elements are."[1]

I first came into contact with Peter Brook's theatre at a workshop organised by his set designer Jean Guy-Lecat in 2005, in Rio de Janeiro. It was a fundamental exercise to look at architecture through another discipline, and to understand the meaning of the word "essential", which, unlike minimalism, is loaded with symbolism.

1 — Brook, Peter, *There Are No Secrets: Thoughts on Acting and Theatre*, London: Methuen Drama, p. 63.

I realised that the critique of the theatrical spaces developed by the Centre international de création théâtrale (CICT), based at the Théâtre des Bouffes du Nord in Paris, could also "apply" to any architectural space. To rethink an architectural programme—in this case, asking "what should a theatre look like?"—is to go back to the very principle of language, of empty space. So it's an exercise that I still use to this day, i.e. to return to the starting point of a brief, with the same phrase: what should a chapel look like? What should a house look like, or a bank?

Then I got to know the work of Polish theatre director Jerzy Grotowski (1933-99), who had a long history of encounters and reciprocities with Peter Brook, and it was key in helping me understand the political and social dimensions of both works.

Grotowski coined the expression "poor theatre", and he eliminated all artificial resources in order to get closer to the essential nature of the discipline. A theatre that abstains from any element other than the actor and the spectator, yet there is still a set design or a reworking of the theatrical space. In his main book *Towards a Poor Theatre* (1968), he describes his thoughts and work: there are no lighting effects, no costumes, no make-up, no music, no other external resources, there is only the naked and essential actor, with his gestures and his "inner impulses". But never does he say that the theatrical space or stage are dispensable. For example, in Pedro Calderón de la Barca's play *The Constant Prince* (1629), the stage is shaped like an arena where only the heads of the audience are visible, almost hidden behind a fence: "From this radically slanted perspective, they look down on the actors [...] like medical students watching an operation."[2]

In both Brook and Grotowski, social and political issues are not only present in the content of the texts, but also in the theatrical space itself. In the case of Peter Brook, he redesigned the Elizabethan theatre, sometimes building temporary theatres on top of existing ones, with the intention of bringing the actor and the audience closer together, and even to share the same floor space. Meanwhile, Grotowski stated that the spectator is in fact more like a witness: "The actors may build structures among the spectators and thus include them in the architecture of action, subjecting them to a sense of the pressure, congestion and limitation of space."[3] Therefore, in both cases, the theatrical space is understood as indivisible from its language.

For Peter Brook's productions, he would find certain spaces (in cities around the world) and add hardly anything to them, not even chairs. In Lisbon, at the convent of Beato António, one diagonal of the cloister was taken up with seats, and the stage was just a rug. In Adelaide, after a long search for a theatre space, he came across a quarry with high earthen walls, and he brought in seats and lighting. In Belgrade, he chose a cinema that was still under construction: "as the cement had just been poured, the surfaces were rough to the touch: the roughness fitted the world of the play very well, with the harshness of tribal life in Uganda".[4] Among

2 — Grotowski, Jerzy, *Towards a Poor Theatre*, London: Muelen, 1969, p. 20 (edited by Eugenio Barba, with a preface by Peter Brook).

3 — *Ibid.*

4 — Todd, Andrew and Lecat, Jean-Guy, *The Open Circle: Peter Brook's Theatre Environments*, London: Faber & Faber, 2003.

many other examples, Peter Brook's theatre appropriated unlikely places in the cities it visited.

Brook's plays were like Marcel Duchamp's *objets trouvés*, i.e. "not a work, but a gesture".[5] Peter Brook set out to build vacuums, so that "the imagination fills the space".[6]

The impermanence and imperfection of theatre are difficult to grasp. It is, perhaps, the most ephemeral art of all. With great effort, through readings and documents, one can imagine what happened in a certain performance. But in truth, it ends there and then, in that very instant. And the only witness is the physical theatrical space, and the memory of those who saw it.

So the idea of impermanence in architecture or in a setting does not exist. All of it will always be part of our cultural world, having existed or not. There is an almost material memory of Grotowski's operating theatre, Aldo Rossi's Teatro del Mondo, and Cedric Price's Fun Palace.

After I had become fascinated with the essential nature of these two theatres and the notion of impermanence, I didn't consider working in an architectural office. I met the architect Gisela Magalhães, who had worked in Brasília with Oscar Niemeyer, and I spent years with her doing exhibition design for historical museums in Brazil. I found the work really engaging, i.e. the process itself of finding historians and philosophers to design an exhibition.

Alongside this, I developed my own residential projects and then worked for the theatre director Bia Lessa, with whom I made Humanidade Pavilion in 2012. This project appropriates temporary scaffolding (prevalent in the Copacabana landscape), and it generated reflections for a series of other projects: the Ministry for All in Brasília, the City Observatory in São Paulo, near Luz station, and the project for a plant nursery on the Flamengo Embankment, which had been Roberto Burle Marx's unrealised dream. These projects only make sense if they are understood as temporary.

Now I am starting a project with a design that appropriates a particular way of doing things: that is, the fragile constructions of the Landless Workers' Movement (the MST: Movimento Sem Terra) and the billboards on the roadsides. They are fragments of pre-existing structures that already form part of the landscape.

The idea is to "occupy" the middle of the coffee fields of Minas Gerais. The entrepreneur Milena Rodrigues has an ongoing social project with the coffee farmers of southern Minas, namely the Flor de Café project, which has brought together small farmers and adds value to their product by selling it directly to various places around the world. The project currently has no budget to build the Coffee Centre

5 — Paz, Octavio, *Marcel Duchamp or El castillo de la pureza*, Mexico City: Ediciones Era, 1968 (English translation: *Marcel Duchamp; or, The Castle of Purity*, London: Cape Goliard P., 1970).

6 — Brook, Peter, *The Open Door: Thoughts on Acting and Theatre*, New York: Theatre Communications Group, 1995.

where there would be classrooms, coffee tasting rooms, a shelter to receive visitors and a museum to retell the colonising history of coffee. This would all be part of a tourist route around the region's agriculture. The last conversation I had with Milena began with a discouraging overview of the current economic and political situation in Brazil, and it ended with a discussion about the MST (the largest social movement in Latin America today, a peaceful movement in which landless farmers seek land to occupy and plant crops, and in which some 300,000 families are involved). The MST build whole cities out of black plastic and wood. The conclusion of our conversation was that we could do the same thing: create a landmark on the terrain, like the MST's cities. I don't think you need a design, just a gesture.

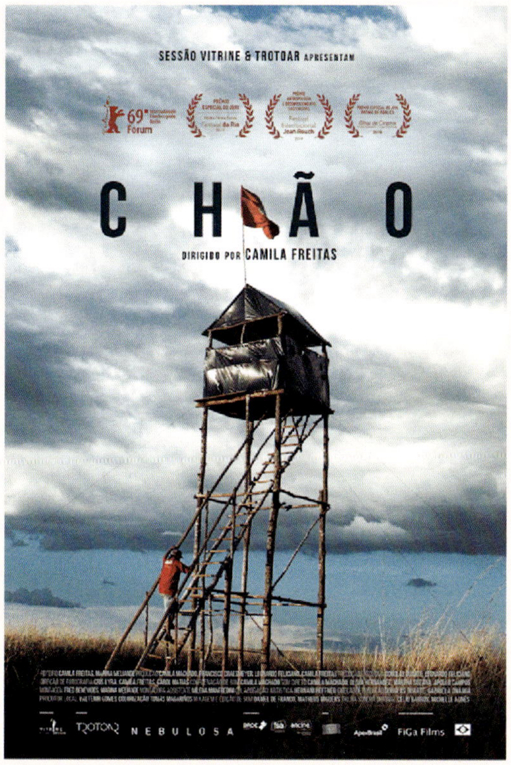

Camila Freitas, *Chão*, 2019.

Given my fascination with the ephemeral—that only the theatre can provide—as a student I opted to work with the architect and set designer Gisela Magalhães, who had previously collaborated with Oscar Niemeyer in the construction of Brasília. Gisela dedicated part of her life to exhibition design, most notably for several major history museums in Brazil, and I ended up working with her for four years. So, I never actually did an internship in any architecture office. As far as I was concerned, Gisela's process of working with historians, philosophers and designers was much more fascinating than any other line of work.

Following that period, I received my first invitations to get involved in exhibition design. I worked on a show about Brazilian jewellery, at the Rio de Janeiro Museum of Modern Art (MAM), where translucent frames were suspended and the jewellery floated upon eight tonnes of small pieces of broken glass, like "crystallised water". At the centre of the exhibition, projections on the floor depicted "hands" digging into

Carla Juaçaba and Leila Rodrigues, exhibition design: *Joias de Chaumet*, National Museum of Fine Arts (MNBA), Rio de Janeiro, 2002

Carla Juaçaba, exhibition design: *Joia Brasil*, Museum of Modern Art (MAM), Rio de Janeiro, 2005

Carla Juaçaba, exhibition design: Children's Room, University of Fortaleza (Unifor), Ceara, 2015

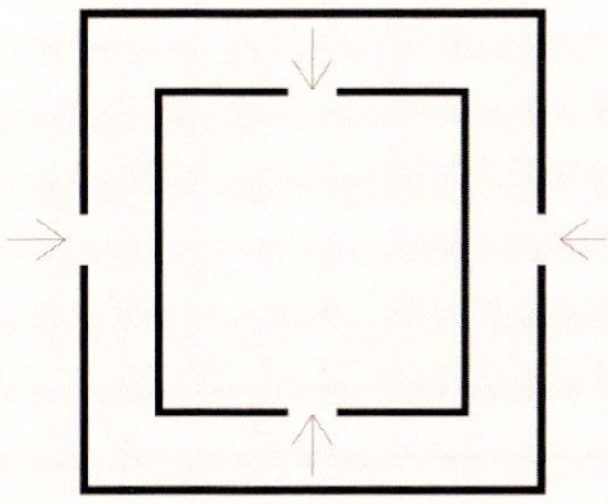

Carla Juaçaba, exhibition design: *A viagem das carrancas,* Moreira Salles Institute (IMS), Rio de Janeiro, 2015-16.

Carla Juaçaba, exhibition design: *Sergio Larraín: um retângulo na mão,* Moreira Salles Institute (IMS), Rio de Janeiro, 2018/ São Paulo, 2019.

Carla Juaçaba, exhibition design: *Visual Natures*, Museum of Art, Architecture and Technology (MAAT), Lisbon, 2022

the earth, looking for precious stones: they represented the *garimpo*, an artisanal mining practice which is now considered harmful to the environment.

I also worked on another jewellery exhibition, this time for Chaumet, which was held at the National Museum of Fine Arts in Rio de Janeiro. The jewels were in fact under water, i.e. a huge water table with showcases inside, which was also a reference to the origin of the precious stone.

The Children's Room has a peculiar story. I visited the atelier of Paulo Mendes da Rocha; he was always in conversation, and I was silent. He described (he didn't show me any drawings) a project he had never built: a house where children enter from everywhere, while the door is for grown-ups only. Later, I made a temporary art room for children: it could be described in that same way.

Furthermore, I designed an exhibition for the Moreira Salles Institute (IMS): it was a display of *carrancas*, i.e. the kind of sculpted wooden figureheads found on the prow of the boats along the São Francisco River. This exhibition theme was first proposed by Lina Bo Bardi in the 1950s, and she said something significant: "I will place the *carrancas* on top, giving them the dignity they deserve, like where they belonged, on the prow of the ships." I found Lina's description to be quite sufficient, so I borrowed her ideas, albeit in a very different design: for this exhibition, the sculptures were placed upon stepped totems, which also served to elevate them.

I went on to design other exhibitions for the Moreira Salles Institute, both in Rio de Janeiro and São Paulo. They were about the Chilean photographer Sergio Larraín, in which the exhibition space alluded to the labyrinthine spaces of the city of Valparaíso.

Biography

Carla Juaçaba

Carla Juaçaba (Rio de Janeiro, Brazil, 1976) has been developing her independent practice in Rio de Janeiro since 2000, and her office is currently engaged in both cultural programmes and private projects. Juaçaba has been teaching at the Academia di Architettura di Mendrisio since 2019. She is also a PhD student at the Madrid School of Architecture (ETSAM-UPM).

Juaçaba is still actively involved in academia, both teaching and research: she has lectured at the GSD (Harvard University), GSAPP (Columbia University) and Academia di Architettura di Mendrisio, among other institutions. She was on the jury for the Ibero-American Architecture and Urbanism Biennial (BIAU) in Madrid (2012 and 2019), and she served as jury president for the 2022 Simon Architecture Prize, Barcelona. In 2013, Juaçaba won the first edition of the arcVision Prize – Women in Architecture, and in 2018 she won *Architectural Review's* Emerging Architecture Award. The model of Juaçaba's Vatican chapel is now part of the collection at the Musée national d'art moderne, Centre Pompidou.